CONTENTS

PREFACE

One day I was sitting with my 16-year-old grandson, Creed, on the tailgate of my red '89 Toyota pickup. He began to share with me his interest in psychology. "Psychology is the scientific study of the human mind and its functions, especially where it comes to affecting behavior", he explained to me. I thought this would be a good time to share some of my supernatural encounters with him. Up until this time, none of my grandchildren knew much about my life and I wanted to share some of the encounters I have experienced facing death in the supernatural.

We all live in two worlds: the natural and the supernatural. Many people do not understand the significance of both these worlds and how they can influence our lives. Both worlds have had a profound effect on me and my life.

I explained to Creed, how I perceived this world and this vast universe of which we are a part. Some can only see the materialistic world in which we live and do not understand the presence of a supernatural world as well.

I found myself in the supernatural world that encompasses the whole universe many times in my life. I have experienced the supernatural world through visions and near-death experiences.

Next to where we were parked, my grandson's dad had dumped a large pile of pea gravel. I picked up a small stone that was lying next to me. Showing it to him I explained, "This represents the earth; the earth is the natural world in which we live." I then threw it into the large pile of pea gravel. "Let us say that the large pile represents the universe; the small stone seems insignificant next to the large mound of gravel."

I was introduced to the unseen world when I was about 5-years old. This is a world that few people know exists. I assure you that these two worlds exist, the world in which we live and another unseen world. The unseen world is controlled by God and the devil, who is called the prince of the world. The devil sits in the heavenly realm with all of his spiritual forces of evil.

"We know that we are children of God, and that the whole world is under the control of the evil one." - 1John 5:19

When I became a born-again believer and turned my life over to the Lord, the Holy Spirit opened my eyes as to how a person can be invaded by a demonic spirit. That person does not necessarily have to be involved in some kind of sin. In my case, the door was opened by many curses that were spoken over me. I've learned through experience how a demon can intertwine itself into someone's personality.

"The devil made me do it!" That humorous saying is somewhat true. Through the years I learned that I had acquired supernatural powers; I could use a Ouija board. I could do handwriting, use a divining rod, and find hidden coins. All these things are found in the supernatural world and are controlled by Satan.

I would like to share my life. How a loving God spared my life numerous lives and was watching over me from birth, preparing me for what he had ahead. **I** did not personally know this loving God during all these events, but I assure you that he knew me.

I especially pray this writing will connect in a powerful way with the ones I so dearly love. My children and grandchildren have never heard all of my story and I want them to always understand how much my life changed when I received the Lord.

When I was about fourteen-years old, I wrote the following poem about this wonderful God who I did not yet know.

A Touch of Mastery by John Kenyon

It's wonderful when you think of it
What God can really do

The way he paints the autumn leaves
And turns the sky so blue
The way He calls the birds to go
When winter is drawing nigh
And how He calls them back again
When warm air blows on high
And in the meadow early
He lets pure water flow
From the many tiny snowflakes
That fell not long ago
With this He breathed a word
And blossoms popped with glee
By this we know it's springtime
The master's hand we see
In every little flower
And every mighty tree

We see His marvelous workings
A touch of Mastery
My prayer is that every person who reads this poem may personally experience a touch of God in his or her life.

CHAPTER ONE
THE EARLY DAYS

This story is true and it's about a loving God who created me. I was born John Dale Kenyon on March 1, 1940, about 1 a.m. at St. Joseph Mercy Hospital in Aurora, IL. My mother's delivery was difficult because I was a breach baby. She always explained that I was born butt first. To my regret I also found myself in the arms of a mother who understood nothing about love. It was not her fault; it was the way she was raised. She never talked much about her upbringing but when she did, I began to put the pieces of this puzzle together. It was not a pretty picture.

The Second World War had begun a year before I was born. At the time, my family lived in a little town called Elburn, about 20 miles from where I was born. The family lived there until I was two-years-old when we moved to Maryland and then to California.

In California my dad got a job in the shipyards wiring up the guns on big battleships. Later he revealed he did this to avoid the draft.

I had two older siblings, a brother and a sister. My brother left home at an early age, so I never really knew him. To this day I believe he did it to escape from our mother. She had an extremely bad temper which she used to discipline her children.

I began to run away from home when I was just a little boy, about the age of 4. After the first time I went missing, my dad built a fence in the backyard hoping this would put a stop to my exploits; it did not. I found a shovel and used it to climb up and over the fence. I stayed out all night and everyone was frantically looking for me.

Early the next morning, my brother spotted me hiding in a field down the street from where we lived. When I got home my mother took me into our garage. She got hold of an army belt and began to beat me with the buckle. My sister, seeing what was happening, tried to help me by grabbing the belt. Instead my mother turned and started beating my sister also. This gave me a chance to run from our mother and into the house where my dad was sleeping before leaving for his night shift job. This is the last thing I remember about this incident except I know if I had not escaped from my mother, I would have died that day.

After three years, our dad moved the family back to Elburn, IL where he started an electrical business but unfortunately it soon failed. He was too trusting with people. Customers would come into his shop where he kept his supplies and take whatever they wanted, but never paid him. Soon after closing shop, he took a job in Geneva, IL working for Averill Electric.

As I have said my mother was physically abusive but she was also verbally abusive. She was a screamer, constantly calling me stupid. After a while I began to believe her. I found myself in first grade with a teacher who was exactly like my mother.

She would come face to face with me and scream when I would miss a spelling word or make any other type of mistake. I was told later the teacher had been admitted to an insane asylum but the abuse she and my mother had inflicted upon me had done its damage.

Next Dad moved our family from Elburn to Geneva into a home on the Fox River. Now about 8-years old, I would go down to the river every day to fish and play. This river became a sanctuary, away from my mother

There was an old, wooden dam about a mile downstream from our house that had partially washed out. The water came only up to my waist. I would often arise at sunrise and go down to this dam where I would meet a friend. Together we would fish and play until it was almost dark. I loved this river and the old, moss-covered dam. We spent many days jumping off the dam onto the slippery boards which we used to slide into the shallow water below. Neither of our parents ever inquired about what we had been doing all day.

At the far end of the dam was a long canal about 150 feet long and 10 feet deep. The canal was attached to an old mill where water would run into a paddle wheel and turn a grinding apparatus. The apparatus was used to grind corn that the farmers would bring in.

I was told that my grandfather was the one who held the patent on this grinder. It was not in use at the time and had been shut down for many years.

My first supernatural escape from death occurred one day when I was walking along the canal. Three boys were swimming in the canal. I did not know how to swim but when one of the boys called to me to jump in; I fool heartedly did and found myself sinking under the water. As I looked up, I could see the sun rays filtering down and I knew I was in trouble.

My lungs started to fill with water and I struggled back to the surface only to find myself sinking again. Somehow, I managed to pull myself to the surface one more time.

This time one of the boys saw that I was in trouble. A large log was floating next to him. As I came up he pushed this log over to me and I was able to grab onto it. His quick thinking saved my life. To this day I do not know who that boy was because I never encountered him again and I've often wondered what the chances were that log was right there at the exact time I needed it. God had his angels watching over me even though I did not yet believe in him.

CHAPTER TWO
HUNTING AND FISHING

In my younger years, I loved to hunt and fish. I still do enjoy fishing but no longer hunt. My favorite hunting spot was along the railroad tracks that ran from my hometown in Geneva to Chicago. I owned a Stevens twenty-gauge shotgun and a slingshot, and was a Cracker Jack shot with either one of them.

Even as a young boy, I was a bit of an entrepreneur. I was always creating ways to make some money. My sister and I would go down to Island Park and climb over a bridge where we'd spend the day on a small island. We enjoyed catching fish and turtles. Occasionally, a beer bottle would float by and I'd wade out and grab it because I could take it to the liquor store uptown where they paid five cents per bottle.

Also I earned money from the city folks who regularly came out from Chicago to fish along the river. I became friends with some of them and they frequently bought my "Secret Formula" dough ball bait which sold for $1 a ball.

The bait was about the size of a baseball, and worked well attracting many species of fish. One time a big, old guy knocked on the back door of our home.

After mom answered it, he uttered, "Is your boy here? I need some of his special bait. By the way, your boy is so smart, I wouldn't be surprised if he grew up to be President of the United States." I caught some huge carp but because people in our area didn't eat them, I sold them to the Chicago crowd. Sometimes the price was as much as $10 for just one fish. That was lots of money back then. From time to time I would sell some of the carp to a nearby bar, which featured a fish fry every Friday night. I was paid good money for my catch but always wondered if their customers understood they were eating carp.

Growing up, my dad would take me hunting or fishing occasionally. This was exciting because I would always catch most of the fish. One day, as we were sitting next to each other in the boat, my dad said to me, "The reason you catch most of the fish is that I have to operate the outboard motor and I always end up with gas on my hands." In my young mind, I felt like that was a valid excuse.

The last time I ever went fishing with my dad was when we went to Canada. I was in great form and caught all the grayling. Dad and my uncle caught nothing. When nightfall came, my uncle fried my fish over the campfire, and we all had a wonderful time together. The memory of spending time with my dad will always be special to me.

My father financially always took care of our family. He was a hard worker and never missed a day of work. In all my troubles, he never stopped being my dad.

At the age of 15, I tried to commit suicide. I realized his great love for me as he stood beside my hospital bed. This was the first time in my life I truly comprehended I had a caring dad.

As the years pass, I have come to realize how committed he was to me; how much he really loved me. At the end of his life, as he lay on his death bed, I heard the words he had always had in his heart. "Dale, I love you."

CHAPTER THREE
MY HITCHHIKING TRIPS

By the time I reached 14 years old I began hitchhiking to get away from my homelife. I hitched a ride to Florida with my older sister. To my delight we ended up in West Palm Beach. By now I had become a pretty good swimmer and I enjoyed the beautiful beaches with clear, blue water.

One day while swimming out off a reef, I met a large hammerhead shark. It didn't take me long to decide to leave the water! I was wearing a mask, snorkel and flippers so I could swim pretty fast.

My next, even more intense encounter that occurred while swimming, was with a giant barracuda. I was swimming in about 10 feet of water off one of the reefs, heading out to deeper water when suddenly the hair stood up on the back of my neck. I sunk down and looked around. To my amazement I felt a huge eye looking straight at me at the end of the reef. I shivered as I sensed its oversized body come up over the reef and move to my right.

To my mind this was a perfect maneuver for its attack. I turned and frantically swam as fast as I could back to shore. Hitting the beach in stride, not wasting time taking off my flippers, I did not stop running until I literally slammed into a palm tree. Two young ladies were sunbathing about 30 yards away and they had a small dog with them. I warned them not to let their dog go into the water. While staying in West Palm Beach, Florida, I had very little food to eat. I would go find a coconut and poke a hole in it and drink out the liquid. As I was starting to tire of always being hungry, I decided to head north up the east coast. My destination was Baltimore, Maryland where I would visit a cousin.

A small library was located about three blocks from my cousin's house and one day I decided to go check it out even though I was not much of a book reader. Despite this fact, I decided to take out a library card. About a week later, I decided to go back to the library to see if they had any books on the occult. I was already acquainted with the unseen world and I had become unquestionably drawn to it. At this time, I did not know too much about what I was getting into and, of course, did not know how dangerous it could become in one's life.

To my surprise, back in a corner I found several books I was looking for. One small book especially drew my attention, it was on the top shelf next to some larger books. Reaching up I took the book in my hand. I read the title and began to thumb through it. One chapter began to reveal the secrets of the universe, I was amazed at what I was reading. I turned the page and the next sentence blew my mind. It said "*stop seeking or you will die*"!

Right then, I thought to myself, "You have got to have this book". Reaching for my library card, I discovered I had left it back at the house. Noticing a librarian working on the other side of the bookshelf, I decided that I would hide the book between two larger volumes and rush back to the house to retrieve my card. Several minutes later I returned to check out my prize book. The librarian was still working in the next aisle over.

As I reached between the two larger volumes, I realized the little book was nowhere to be found. I walked around to where the librarian was working and asked her if anyone had been back in the area since I had left; she said "no". I then walked up to the librarian who was standing at the front desk and asked her the same question.

She responded that no one had come in since I had earlier. This experience was impossible to explain; it was most strange. I looked at it as a warning of some kind. Perhaps it was one of the pieces of a puzzle I would put together down the road.

Soon after this encounter I began to experience some paranormal phenomenon. One evening as we were finishing up dinner at my cousin's house, I told him about my experience at the library and my interest in the occult. He asked me if I'd ever tried handwriting, but I did not know what that meant. He instructed me to take a piece of paper, lay it on the table, then take a pencil in my hand and place it on top of the paper. Then he asked me a question. To my amazement, the pencil began to move on its own and correctly answered his question. I was deeply impressed.

A couple weeks later I wound up in Greenwich Village in New York, NY. Soon after arriving, I met a curator at one of the art galleries and we instantly seemed to hit it off. I was interested in becoming an artist so we had common interests. He asked if I would like to stay with him for a couple of weeks. Of course, I said yes.

After a short time; however, I moved on and it wasn't until several years later I got a news clipping from my cousin saying the art curator had been murdered. This was not surprising as he had shared some secrets about his life and about some of the people he hung out with. He had dark dealings I cannot reveal.

Next, I decided to go to Norfolk, VA to visit my aunt. She worked for one of the naval officers at the Norfolk Naval Base. By that time, it was getting close to the fall school enrollment so I decided I had better hitchhike back to Illinois. My aunt wanted me to stay and live with her but I decided it was best to go home.

When I got to the Pennsylvania turnpike, I ran into a little trouble with the state police. It was late in the afternoon; I was on the freeway walking along when a state trooper pulled up behind me. He stepped out and asked me where I was going. I told him I was heading to Illinois. He then informed me that it was illegal to hitchhike on the Pennsylvania turnpike and motioned me to get into his vehicle before heading to the Police headquarters.

When he got to the station, he asked me if my parents knew where I was. Of course, I said yes. He turned and asked me for their home phone number which I gave him; he proceeded to call them. By this time, it was getting late into the afternoon. My dad answered the phone. I heard the officer ask if he knew where his son was. My dad replied that I was somewhere between Virginia and Illinois.

The officer asked what he should do with me. My dad asked if he could put me on a bus but the officer informed him I had only $6.00. My dad grumbled, "Then do whatever". After hanging up, the patrolman loaded me back into the police car. He then proceeded to drive me to the state line. It was dark by the time we arrived. He pulled off on an old road where he left me out. There was one overhead street light and I really felt like I had been left in the middle of nowhere. I could see the turnpike from where I was standing, but I could not get to it from where I was.

I stood alone for about an hour, hoping someone would come by and pick me up. Finally, headlights pierced the dark, lonely area and I began waving my hands.

The time was 1a.m. but the car stopped anyway. The door opened and I looked in. To my surprise, 7 Mexicans were sitting in back looking at me. One of them waved me in and squeezed me into the front seat.

I had an old backpack with me that had a zipper on it. One of them took my pack and threw it into the back seat. When I heard the zipper open, I knew they were looking through it but wouldn't retrieve anything of value. Several miles down the road they were turning off. The driver stopped the car and I opened the door as one of them handed me my pack. I thanked them and they went on their way.

I found myself again on a seldom traveled road. It wasn't long until a Mayflower moving truck came along, stopped and picked me up. He asked where I was headed and I told him Chicago. He said great, he was going there also. When we got to Chicago, he opened the back and let me out.

After thanking him I went on my way back to Geneva. It was an odd coincidence that about three years later I met him again when I was helping a friend move. He remembered me! What a small world we live in.

When I got home, my parents did not ask me where I had been, but they seemed glad to see me.

CHAPTER FOUR
OUT WEST

In fall, I enrolled in Geneva High School as a freshman. I did not enjoy school much. Many days I would look out the school window and wish summer was here. I did like sports so I went out for football. The school had so few students, forcing us to play varsity football because not enough boys were available to make a junior varsity team. I played center linebacker and left half back. I also played safety and held the football at kick off.

When spring came, I went out for track. I placed third in all three events I entered. Our school was competing against five different schools. One day at practice, I got into a fight with the track and field coach. I was so mad that I threw my track shoes at him and left. I never went back to Geneva High School.

After quitting high school, I decided to take a trip out west. My real intention was to hitchhike to Alaska. Before I left, I had a small book of the New Testament in my bedroom. In the back it also had the Psalms. I opened up to the 23rd Psalm, *"The Lord is my Shepherd"*. I was never good at memorizing but for some reason I decided to memorize it and have never forgotten it.

It was a Saturday morning as I started my journey walking out of town. A friend of mine pulled up in his car. He asked me where I was going and I told him I was going to Alaska. As he pulled away, he wished me good luck.

I never took much with me when I hitchhiked, only what was on my back. This time, I had a small satchel with a pair of socks, shorts and shirts and the small New Testament. I never took any food or water as it was too heavy and took up too much room. I hitchhiked west on Hwy 90-94 and I turned onto US 90 towards South Dakota. From that point I wound up in Billings, Montana.

I stopped at a little pizza place. The man who owned it used to play for the Chicago Cubs. We hit it off and he asked if I would like to work for him in his pizza parlor. For some reason I said yes. He shared with me his future plans of opening another restaurant and asked if I would like to be the manager. Without hesitation I agreed; however, our relationship would soon change.

I had never worked a cash register before, and I had to teach myself how to count out change. Friday nights were pretty busy and I remember one night I had mischarged one of our customers. It was about $16. I corrected his bill and re-rang it, but I neglected to take the mistake off the cash register.

The owner had given me a little room to sleep in at the restaurant. Coming out of my room on Saturday morning, the owner and his girlfriend were sitting at a table on the other side of the restaurant. They called me over and accused me of stealing $16. I told them I was not a thief and I did not take any money from them. I had been falsely accused; I took some of my tip money and threw it at them. It was all in silver dollars.

Years later, when I owned my own business, I realized the mistake I had made. As I've said before, I did not know how to operate a cash register. Looking back on all this, I realized that God had wanted me to move on. He had a plan mapped out for my life. It is so wonderful when God replaces something painful with His own plan. God has a primary concern for all of His children.

Leaving the restaurant, I looked to the hills outside of Billings, MT. They were about two miles away. I thought I would go up to one of the hills and sit on the hillside and read my little Bible. To my dismay, a swiftly running river separated me from the hills. Later I found out it was the Yellowstone River. This was the river that I was about to forge.

Having lived on the Fox River most of my life, I was not afraid of water. There was a small island in the middle of this river and on the other side was approximately an 8-foot high, dirt bank. Because the far end the river curved around the island, I could not see what was below. I took off my shoes and hung them around my neck as I headed out towards the end of the island. The rocks under the water became very slippery.

As I crossed the end of the island, the water became deeper, about up to my thighs. It was moving very fast. I thought that if I was swept downstream, I could swim to the other bank and climb out.

At that moment I walked into the supernatural. I felt a hand grab me by the shoulder and listened to an audible voice say, "Turn back or you will die". I hastily turned and headed back to the other bank wondering what was going on. Could it have been an angel that had warned me? I believe it was! I looked up the river and saw a bridge about a quarter-mile upstream.

My curiosity got the best of me, so I went up to the bridge and crossed over to the other side. As I walked to the other end of the island, I was astounded to lay eyes upon a huge whirlpool with logs as large as telephone poles whirling around in it. To this day I still shudder at what would have happened if I had not obeyed the voice. I would have disappeared off the face of this earth. I probably would have been ground up for fish food. Only God knew where I was.

It was starting to get dark so I decided to walk over to the highway that would take me back down into town. Soon it was almost pitch black. As I was walking down the road, I began to hear some fearsome sounds like snarling and growling off in the desert. I soon realized the howling and barking sounds were coming straight at me.

I listened intently as the sounds came closer. It was a pack of wild dogs and they were coming straight for me; I stood frozen, waiting. Suddenly the lights of a car came down the road. I was hoping the driver of the car would see what was happening and stop to pick me up. As the animals came closer, the car lights began to reflect on the animals' red eyes. Their flashing eyes and gnashing teeth looked like something straight out of a horror movie.

As both the car and the dog pack came closer, I thought what was I to do? I realized the car was not going to stop and rescue me. A thought popped into my head: when the lights of the car moved closer, I would raise my arms and charge at the dogs while screaming at the top of my voice. That is what I did! My shadow looked like some kind of ferocious monster coming straight at them. Instantaneously, those frightened canines turned tail and sped back into the desert. I thought to myself, "No way could this be happening"? How could everything have worked out at the exact moment I needed it. I know God's angels were on high alert.

At night, the temperature began to drop; it would be very uncomfortable and I had nowhere to stay that night. Coming back into town, I noticed a large off-the-road tire standing outside of a store. I went over to investigate it. The inside of this large tire was shaped somewhat like a hammock and I thought this could be a good place to spend the night.

I crawled in; it didn't feel too bad. Because I was small, my body seemed to fit very comfortably inside the tire. Boy, what a mistake I made! I had not observed the large amount of rubber dust that was inside the tire. Night had fallen and it was dark outside. I sure noticed it in the morning when I woke up at about 5 a.m. The rubber dust was all over me; I looked like a chunk of coal.

By luck, the local Laundromat was about a block down the road and it was open. I peered into the window to see if anyone was inside. To my delight, it was vacant. I rushed inside and began stripping off my outer clothes. Thank goodness I still had some tip money. I threw my clothes into a washer and dropped in some coins. In the back. was a small sink holding a little dish with some soap in it. It also had a paper towel dispenser. How fortunate I was to have these things at my disposal. Without them, I would have had a hard time cleaning myself up.

Several minutes later two ladies walked in with their laundry. I was in the back with only my underpants on. To my relief they seemed to ignore me. I heard the washer shut off so I rushed and took my clothes out of the washer and threw them into the dryer. The women again, didn't seem to notice. As soon as my clothes were dry, I grabbed them out and began to put them on. In short order I exited the building and decided it was time to move on. I stayed on I-90 until it intersected with I-5 North. I wound up in Everett, Washington.

Upon arrival, I was stopped by some border agents. When they asked me where I was going; I told them I was on my way to Alaska. They informed me to cross into Canada, I needed $50 and a sponsor. It was illegal to cross the border without these things, so that was the end of one of my grandiose dreams.

Next, I headed down to Seattle. I started back east on US-90 and got a ride all the way to Missoula which is the beginning of the Bitterroot Mountains. I don't remember how I got on the downside of these mountains but it was a very lonely road with little traffic. To my dismay, the weather was bitterly cold, and I was soon overtaken by a huge snowstorm. It was not long before I was waist-deep in snow. I was wearing only a Levi jacket, Levi pants and tennis shoes, with no place to take shelter from the blizzard.

I could barely see in front of me because it was snowing so hard. As I was trudging along, I bumped into something; it was a vehicle. As I felt my way around it, I realized it was a snowplow. It must have broken down and the crew had abandoned it. I stepped up onto the running boards, opened the door and crawled into the cab. By this time, it was early morning.

The next thing I remembered was the squeaky door opening and a surprised crew member staring at me. The first thing he said was

"Where in the world did you come from?" I could faintly speak; I was shaking so badly from the cold. I was in a stage of hypothermia. My teeth chattered and I shivered so forcefully I could not sit still. They loaded me into another snowplow and headed down the mountain, dropping me off at gas station in the town of Butte, MT. I know that if the crew would have shown up just 20 minutes later; they would have found a corpse lying in the cab. Looking back, I knew in my mind that someone was watching over me. Later in my life, it became apparent it was a loving God.

My God knew me even before my life began. (Jeremiah1:5) "Before I formed you in the womb, I knew you."

The gas station was open when I arrived. A gentleman walked out the door and invited me in. I was still shaking a lot so he offered me a chair to sit down. Sensing I was hungry he handed me a lunch which his wife had packed him. Then, he said he would go next door where there were some small cabins and ask the proprietor if he would let me use one of them to warm up. The proprietor agreed and as we entered the cabin, I noticed it had a small gas furnace.

As he turned it on, he warned me not to turn it up. He said it would get intensely hot inside. I was so cold; I couldn't help myself. As soon as he left, I turned the heat up. I laid down on the bed and covered up. I woke up about an hour later profusely sweating. I jumped up and turned down the heat. After grabbing my little satchel, out the door I went. It had gotten quite a bit warmer outside.

As I was walking along, I spied a grocery store up ahead. I had no money to buy food, so I decided to go behind the store and look into their dumpster to see what I might find to eat. I found some half ripe bananas that someone had discarded. As I reached in to retrieve them, the back door opened and over me towered the manager. He asked me what I was up to and I told him I was hungry. He waved me inside the store and motioned me to follow him. He went behind the counter and took out some cheese. He then grabbed a loaf of bread and put both items into a grocery sack. As he handed me this precious parcel, he said: "I hope this will help you". I was so grateful. I thanked him and left the store. marveling at what had just happened.

As I walked along eating my cheese sandwich, I realized how thirsty I had become. By this time, I was far out of town. It seemed as though no one would stop to pick me up. As time went by, I found myself in a desert-like setting. After a while, I became desperate. I decided to step off the road and pray. I remember kneeling down and crying out to God for help. My prayer was, "Please Lord, send someone who will pick me up". That prayer was answered in about five minutes.

As I walked back to the road, I soon laid eyes on what appeared to be a "half car - half truck" coming in the distance. Two old folks were sitting in it. Pulling over, the couple waved me to jump in. They shared some water with me and down the road we went. As we drove along, they asked me where I was heading. I said that I was going home. They told me they were heading back to their sheep ranch after making their monthly trip to purchase supplies.

The woman then asked if I would like to come out to the ranch and work for them for a while. I inquired how far off the main road was their ranch located. Their reply was - about 24 miles. I thought to myself, that's too far way to be stranded in a desert. I politely declined the offer. I said I needed to return home to begin writing a book about my many adventures.

The old lady in her sweetest voice said, "We have a 16-year-old daughter who lives with us". I didn't take the bait! They soon got ready to turn onto an old dirt road that led to the ranch. I thanked them and said I would remember them in my book.

The next thing I can remember was getting a ride with a truck driver. From that point on I cannot remember how I made it back home. I do remember when I came into town, I met the same friend I had met going out of town. When he asked me where I'd been, I told him I had hitchhiked to the west coast and back. I got into his car and he drove me home. My parents never asked me where I'd been, and I never told them.

CHAPTER FIVE
DANGEROUS ESCAPADES

Some of my escapades were foolish and even dangerous. My friend, Keith, and I used to buddy around together most of the summer on the Fox River. We liked to spend time catching pigeons nesting under the railroad trestle which crossed over the Fox River. The trestle was about sixty feet above the Fox River and the water that ran under it was shallow, about two feet deep. There was not nearly enough water to stop a person's fall if they accidentally fell from the trestle. The trestle was held up by a series of concrete pilings.

We had to climb down a ladder and then navigate a four-inch L-shaped steel beam that crisscrossed the trestle from one piling to the next. It was like walking a tightrope to reach to those birds! With nothing to hold on to, so we had to carefully maintain our balance or face a terrible accident.

One day while on our quest for pigeons, Keith and I had a harrowing experience. For some reason that day I warned Keith to be exceedingly careful and to never, never look down. I led the way that day and was almost up to the first piling when I caught wind of a terrible shriek behind me. Looking back, I gazed upon Keith dangling from one arm. He was grasping the beam with just one hand and wouldn't be able to hold on for long.

I shouted, "Throw your leg up over the beam and pull yourself up!". Keith was an athletic young man and had enough strength to hoist himself to safety. We continued as if nothing had happened. To us, this was all great fun! As an adult, I realize how dangerous this was. No one knew what we were doing or even where we were.

Another time, my friend Roy and I planned a canoe trip down the Fox River to the Illinois River, then to the Mississippi River and ending in New Orleans. A big obstacle was that it was mid-December and cold outside. The Fox River was almost frozen over but that fact didn't deter us at all.

We were convinced we would make a great team, so we packed up all the gear we thought we needed and set out for this adventure. We were in an Old Town canoe my mother had bought for me years ago. It was an exceedingly stable, wide beam, sixteen-foot model. The canoe was one of my prized possessions.

Starting, we needed to break the ice to move to the middle of the river and from that point we headed south. Several times along the way, we had to portage around the dams we encountered. When we arrived in Oswego, we discovered a break was present on one end of the dam. The escaping water was swiftly flowing through it and we could see large timbers rolling and popping up out of the swirling water. Because it was getting late in the afternoon, and we were beginning to tire, we had to make a snap decision whether to portage or take a chance and run through the break in the dam.

We had no life jackets and we understood hitting any of those gigantic timbers would capsize our canoe and dump us into that cold, frigid water. Choosing to forge ahead, our hearts thumping in our chests, we barreled through all that debris and made it safely to our next destination, which was a small island downstream. We spent the night and continued in the morning.

After paddling a while, I observed a Canadian goose floundering in the water. It had been shot by someone, but only wounded. We would need to eat soon so we put it out of its misery and were grateful to have meat for supper. After enjoying a tasty meal, we wrapped the remaining uncooked meat in a newspaper and stowed it away in the canoe. We figured it would keep well because it was still very cold outside. After some time, we reached Yorkville, where we camped. We boiled the remaining bird as soon as we settled in and in our haste didn't allow enough time for it to thoroughly cook.

In no time at all, Roy was doubled over, clutching his stomach and profusely throwing up. When his sheet-white body collapsed to the ground, I thought he might die. I was alarmed! I bundled him up and laid him atop his sleeping bag. After a long and restless night, he awoke feeling much better.

We scanned the area and noticed a barge parked along the riverbank. It would be leaving soon because it was attached to a tugboat. A deckhand was standing nearby so I walked on over and asked him if we could hitch a ride with them down to Peoria, Illinois. He helped us lift our canoe aboard and we were on our way.

The barge was short a deckhand and the captain asked me if I would be interested in the job. I declined his offer for several good reasons. The first was that one of the crew members told me the fellow I would be replacing had just suddenly disappeared without a trace. Secondly, when I asked the captain how and when I would get paid, he replied, "I will set up an account for you at one of the banks along the river so you can just go and withdraw some money whenever you want." This idea sounded fishy to me.

When we landed in Peoria, Roy and I exited that barge. We were ready to head home, so Roy stayed with the canoe while I left to search for transportation back. Here again, God showed me His great favor! Just a few blocks down the street, I came upon a used car dealership. Sitting in the lot, was an old car that looked like it could be in my price range. I went inside to inquire about the vehicle and the dealer noted, "This is a good running car and I will sell it to you for $75." I rapidly agreed. To my amazement, he offered to leave the dealer's plates on the car so I could go home. I promised to removed them when I got to Illinois because they were due to expire on January first. We loaded up the canoe and headed straight for home. We arrived home one day before Christmas. Once again, my parents didn't ask me where I had been or what I had been doing.

One time, a friend and I decided it would be fun to take a swim in the Fox River. We would start by wading out on the top of the dam. I had a history with this dam as it was here where I faced death earlier in my life. The old wood structure had been since replaced with a new concrete one. It was structured in such a fashion that people called it "Killer Dam". Water flowed over the dam and straight down to the bottom of the river. It shot back with great force, causing the effect of a wheel going backward. Anything caught in this circular motion had no way of release.

It had been a rainy season, so the water was dangerously high. At this time, I made another poor choice. I decided to jump out over the raging water and to hopefully land out in the river. Unfortunately, as I jumped, the water grabbed me like a giant hand pushing me back towards the dam. I felt the force of the water sucking me down into the depths of the river. I was determined to survive and struggled back to the surface. I was gasping for air and was pulled under again and again. I was in a large spinning wheel with no way of escape. I developed a plan whereby when the pressure of the downflow of the water forced me to the bottom of the river again, I would touch feet-first. I would then squat down, expelling all the air out of my lungs, and then push upward as hard as I possibly could. I was hoping to thrust myself up and over the wall of water.

Everything needed to come together like clockwork in order for this plan to work. Now the time was right. As my feet hit the bottom of the river, I thrust myself upward. At the very moment I reached the surface, I felt something or someone hit me hard on my back. It propelled me out into the river and away from the dam.

When I was able to look around, I was awestruck as my friend swam up next to me. I asked him why he jumped in and did he realize I was in trouble?" He replied, "No, I thought you were just kidding around." "I didn't jump on purpose. I started to slip off the dam and had to jump."

He had been standing on the three-hundred-foot, long dam with water running around his feet and between his legs. At the exact moment he slipped off the dam, I came up over the crest of the water that was pushing me back towards the dam. He landed right on top of me. His momentum was strong enough to push both of us out into the river.

I asked myself what is the possibility of this happening at the exact time I needed help? It saved my life. I am convinced God watches over those whom He is calling into His kingdom.

1 Corinthians 1:8 - "He will also keep you firm to the end, so that you will be blameless on the day of our Lord Jesus Christ."

CHAPTER SIX
MORE TRAVELS

My next adventure was a trip to Florida with a girlfriend whom I had been dating for ten months. I had just gotten my driver's license and my dad had bought me an old 1932 Chevy from my brother for $150. It was an oil burner, a real junk by today's standards. Dad told me if I ever got a speeding ticket, he would take the car away from me. Of course, I got a ticket for speeding; doing 35 mph in a 25 mph zone. I only had temporary license plates on the car and with my irrational line of thinking, not wanting to lose my wheels, I decided to run away to Florida.

I made the mistake of telling my girlfriend what I was about to do. She insisted I take her with me and grabbed my wallet lying on the seat. "Unless you take me with you, I won't give you your wallet back", she threatened". Like a foolish teenager, I agreed.

We left for Florida with only the clothes on our backs. I didn't have much money with me, but despite that, we made it to Florida. I looked in my rearview mirror and observed a police car on my tail.

Sure enough, he started flashing his lights at me. I pulled over and rolled down my window. He asked me for my ID and where we were going.

The officer told me he stopped me because I had no license plates on the vehicle. I told him I had a temporary license plate on my back window. He asked me if our parents knew where we were. He then asked for their phone numbers.

After the officer called our parents, we were both hauled off to the county jail where we stayed until our parents flew down to pick us up. My girlfriend's dad flew them back, while my dad and I drove home.

When we arrived home, I went before a judge. He kindly exonerated me from the speeding ticket after my dad told him what had happened. My girlfriend and I both had to go to a family counselor and tell our story. After hearing our stories, our counselor decided it was best we should break off our relationship, which I agreed to. It didn't matter how much I tried to stay away from her, my girlfriend would not leave me alone. My dad had to go before a judge to issue a restraining order against her. This stopped her harassment and protected me from seeing her again.

My next exposure to death was on a Sunday afternoon. We had just finished a big family dinner where I remember eating a large amount of food, when a fight broke out between my sister's husband and I. I do not remember what the fight was about, but I do remember becoming unreasonably upset.

Because of all the things that had happened in my young life, I decided it was no longer worth living.

I walked uptown to a corner drugstore and bought a bottle of ant poison. Around the corner was an old building where I used to pick up newspapers to deliver on my paper route. I walked in the side door, opened the bottle of poison and began to drink it. After drinking it, I began to feel sick.

Right then, I heard a car pull up outside, so I ran to the door and looked out. To my amazement, a friend of mine was sitting in his car with the motor running. After I explained to him what had happened, he motioned me in and he rushed me to the hospital which fortunately was only about six blocks away. He then helped me into the emergency room where I was met by two doctors. I told them what I had done and they swiftly began to pump out my stomach. Had my friend not shown up at that perfect time, I probably would have died.

Before I left the hospital, I overheard a doctor tell my dad it was a miracle my stomach had not been burned out. After this whole ordeal, my mother and father decided I should see a psychiatrist. After hearing my story, the psychiatrist told my dad it was not me, but my mother who needed counseling. We never went back.

In spring, my dad asked me if I would like to go to work up in the Canadian province of Saskatchewan. At the time, I had an uncle who lived in Calgary, Alberta Canada. He was the CEO of Shell Oil Company. My dad flew us up to meet my uncle. who flew me to Saskatchewan in his private plane.

I found myself in a prairie-like setting and working for Shell Oil. Shell had a large drilling operation in this area. I was introduced to the foreman and my uncle left. My first assignment was working in the rig shack. This is where most of the tools were kept. I also helped to clean up the rigs that came in from the oil fields which included repainting them.

I found a boarding house in the town where some of my co-workers stayed. I did not last long. I realized why these men were nicknamed roughnecks. Somehow, they found out how much I was earning per hour. Eighteen years of age was the requirement to work for this company; I was sixteen and looked about fourteen. I started at $1.50 an hour and they were making about $1.60 an hour. This made them very upset with me.

One day, I was working with some of the men cleaning up one of the rigs that came in. It was an oppressively hot day and I decided to remove the boots I was wearing. I took them off and set them behind me. The next thing I smelled was burning leather. I looked back and spotted one of the welders with a torch burning up my only pair of boots. Everyone was laughing. Believe me, I did not think it was funny!

I walked over to the rig shack and laid on the floor. The next thing I observed was the same welder standing over me with an oil can. It was the kind that could squirt out oil about 10 feet. I remember looking at him and saying, "don't do it" but he did it any way! He shot oil from my crotch to my head. I jumped up, looked around and spotted a gallon paint can about half full of black machinery paint.

I grabbed it up and yelled, "Don't do that again". He did and I charged at him with the can of paint. As I got close, I threw it on him and dropped the can running for the door. I saw him pick up the paint can and start after me. We were in a fenced enclosure, but I was confident I could outmaneuver him. About a half-hour later he cornered me and grabbed me by the arm, then he proceeded to dump what was left in the can over my head.

It was getting close to quitting time, so I left the yard and headed for the boarding house. By the time I got to the house the paint had already dried on my head. The woman at the boarding house was horrified when she laid eyes on me. She quickly took me into the kitchen and began to cut the hair off of my head. I was shocked when I looked in my bedroom mirror and saw myself completely bald.

Even though my rent was paid up for a month, I left the boarding house and never went back. I moved into an old rig shack I found out in the desert. Someone had left a dirty mattress on the floor that I slept on.

One day while I was walking along the road, I spotted a canister full of kerosene. I was hoping it would work to keep me warm at night. When I lit it up the smoke was so bad it ran me out of the shack.

That week, I went to town and bought a tent and a hat to cover my bald head. My tent did not work out so well and I finally wound up selling it to one of the roughnecks for fifty dollars. I was still working at the yard but after work, I would go exploring.

When darkness fell, I would go into town in back of one of the stores and find a box to sleep in.

Sometimes when I ran out of money, I would go behind a restaurant and rummage through their garbage can to see what I could find to eat. In Canada, restaurants didn't waste much food and threw very little in the trash. I witnessed an example one night while I was looking for some food. I peeked into the kitchen and watched as one of the waitresses scraped some leftover off a customer's plate into a large pot simmering on a stove. Their menu advertised "free soup" with every meal.

During this time in my life, I was searching for God. I came across a small church one night where they were holding some evening meetings and I could hear singing inside. I walked up some stairs into the back of the church where two, young evangelists were speaking. I don't remember anything that they said, but I do remember being invited up to the front of the church to receive what they said was a baptism of the spirit.

Just before I was invited up, an offering plate was passed around. All I had in my pocket was the $50 bill from the tent sale. I took the bill out and threw it in the offering plate. I then went up to the altar. I experienced a strange sense come over me; something took hold of my tongue and it began to move on its own. At that moment the man standing behind me slapped me on my back. He screamed, "Receive the Holy Ghost". Talk about being freaked out; like a shot I turned around and ran for the back door.

I was standing on the back porch when the two evangelists walked out. They were overjoyed that someone had left a $50 bill in the offering. For some reason, one of them looked at me and inquired, "Were you the one who gave the $50?' I said yes. To this day I don't know why they thought it was me. One of them even offered to give it back. Of course, I said, "No--I want you to have it". They were delighted.

It was a beautiful night as I walked out into the desert. The stars looked like bright, shining diamonds set in the heavens.

I remember kneeling down and looking out into this vast universe. I cried out, "If there's a God in heaven, show me the true religion". The next day, my dad called me at work and said he was sending me money to take the train home. I told him when I got home, I wanted to find a Christian school to go to.

CHAPTER SEVEN
BACK TO SCHOOL

By the time I got home, my mother had enrolled me in a Seventh Day Adventist school, in Broadview, IL, about 35 miles from my home in Geneva. I had to start my freshman year all over again. The Academy was a boarding school where pupils lived at school nine-months of the year and were allowed to go home for summer break.

I moved into one of their dorms where I shared a room with another student. The school rules were very strict and I believe I broke every one of them. Playing with a Ouija board was strictly forbidden. Somehow, I got a hold of one and brought it to school. One night, my roommate and I were asking the Ouija board questions. It would not work for my roommate and only worked for me.

Late one night there was a noise at our door. I looked out where I observed a frightened-looking boy who had been listening to what we were doing. I was so pumped that I reached out and grabbed him by his neck, lifting him off the floor.

He found himself dangling in the air up against the wall. I warned him not to say anything to anyone about this incident as it might lead to expulsion.

The next day, I heard he had called his mother to come pick him up. I never saw him again. I was never questioned about what had happened that night. Here again, God was showing his favor to me.

During summer when school let out, I thought I would try selling some Seventh Day Adventist books to help pay for my next year's tuition. It did not work out, so I decided to hitchhike to Paducah, Kentucky where an uncle lived. He and his wife lived on a small farm out in the country with his two daughters. I never told my parents where I was going. I just left. This would be one of the places where I would face death again.

One morning my uncle asked me if I would like to plow a field. It was a piece of bottomland he was sharecropping with his neighbor. This piece of bottomland was surrounded by three deep ditches. I had never driven a tractor before, so I was excited about the offer and readily agreed to help. It seemed like quite an adventure to me, but it turned out to be a nightmare.

As I was plowing, I heard a voice say, "Be careful. The devil is trying to kill you". I looked around and watched a large thundercloud coming up over the horizon. I thought to myself, if I got struck by lightning, I would be well-grounded. This tractor had big, rubber tires and the plow was in the ground.

For some reason, I began to speed up. Coming up to the ditch, I began to make a turn. Suddenly, the front end rose up like a wild stallion and I realized the plow had gotten hung up on something. This made the tractor jump wildly.

The next thing I remember was waking up. Apparently, I had been knocked unconscious. The tractor had landed upside down in the ditch and I found myself pinned under the large back fender.

The motor was still running, and the back tires were still turning. My body was only inches from these large spinning tires. I reached up trying to grab them, hoping they would stop.

The tractor motor finally died, and the tires stopped moving. Somehow my foot had gotten caught up in the steering column and my body was violently thrown under the tractor. I found that my body had landed right in the middle of a muskrat slide, a spot where a muskrat would slide off a bank, making a big rut. If my body had not landed as it did, I would have been crushed under the weight of the large tractor tire. A foot in either direction, and I would have been killed.

Since I was pinned under the fender, I decided I'd try to dig my way out. To my horror, it started to rain, and I became frightened. My uncle had told me that when water enters ditches, water moccasins come out to hunt for prey. He had tales of children being bitten by the snakes. The only option I had was to try to dig myself out from under the fender as speedily as possible.

In a short time, I was able to free my foot from the steering column. I then began to dig along the right side of my body. The clay dirt was soft and I was able to free myself. As I stood up, I realized I had sprained my ankle. I also identified a large dark blood clot on the side of my waist. Other than that, nothing was broken.

I began to limp back to the farmhouse. My uncle and a neighbor were sitting on the back porch. As I approached, my uncle hollered out, "Is everything ok?"

I shook my head no. Coming up to the porch he caught sight of me limping and asked me what had happened. I told him the tractor had flipped over in the ditch on top of me. He hurriedly helped me into his truck and we headed for the doctor.

Back then hospitals had no emergency room so I was taken straight in to see the doctor. After examining me, he found nothing was wrong except for the sprained ankle and bruises. The physician told us a week earlier, a farmer had flipped over on his tractor and was killed. He looked at me in amazement, realizing I could have suffered the same fate.

My uncle and I headed back to the accident site where the farmer had brought in a crane to lift the tractor out of the ditch. He attached some chain to the tractor and lifted it straight up out of the ditch, set it over on the ground upside down and then rolled it over onto its wheels. My uncle walked over and looked in the ditch. He detected the imprint of my body where I had fallen into that muskrat slide. He could even see the wrinkles from the pants I was wearing embedded in the clay.

Summer was about over and I needed to head back north to Broadview Academy for my sophomore year. When I arrived at the Academy, I was informed I was not qualified to start my sophomore year. My math teacher, Roy Smith told me I had not taken my final, mandatory algebra exam . I informed Mr. Smith that I comprehended nothing about Algebra. He told me it was ok and to go ahead and take the test anyway.

After he handed me the exam, I began to look at those strange numbers and had no idea what they meant. I guessed something for each answer, but I don't remember what or why. The next day Mr. Smith informed me he was passing me through. He never told me whether I had passed the test.

Mr. Roy Smith was a wonderful man, as were all my teachers. They all showed me unconditional grace and mercy. They were to me at that time - in my young life - the most loving, merciful, and gracious people; slow to judge and quick to forgive my bad behavior. I could have been kicked out of school so many times had it not been for this group of adults who took an interest in me and provided to me all those things that were lacking in my own home. Each one of them in their own way helped me achieve my education and a high school diploma.

Between my sophomore and junior year, I wanted to take on a new adventure. I decided I would join the Navy and found myself at Great Lakes Naval Station in Chicago, Illinois in boot camp. To my horror, I soon found out the officers were very abusive to the recruits. Officers would get in the recruits' faces and scream at them. It reminded me of my mother so I sensed I would not make it through the six weeks. I went before our commanding officer and asked for a discharge. He questioned me as to my request and I told him my story. He graciously accepted it and gave me a general discharge. I decided not to go back to Broadview, instead moving home again.

Later that year, I was accepted into the Chicago Academy for Fine Arts. It was a miracle and only by God's grace I was accepted because one requirement was to have a high school diploma which I did not have. I rode the commuter train forty-five miles from Geneva to Chicago 5 days a week.

At that time, I also took a job in Chicago working from 3:30 p.m. until midnight at Morrows Nut House (My wife has been known to quip how I was well qualified for that job). Because art classes dismissed at 3:00 p.m., I had to hustle to make it to State Street to work on time. I'd spend the evening selling the tastiest nuts anyone ever sampled. At midnight, I locked up and ran down the street as fast as my legs would carry me so I could catch the last train out of the city. It left promptly at 12:30.

On occasion, to my dismay and horror I missed the last train out. If you have ever been stuck in Chicago after midnight, you know that it is not a comfortable place to be, but I had a back-up plan. Another train station a few blocks further away called Union Station, ran all night from Chicago to Aurora. One of its stops was in a small town called Naperville where I had a former girlfriend who I met at Broadway Academy. She still liked me a lot and was always glad to see me no matter what time of the night I showed up. She lived with her parents who also welcomed me. They were a genuinely kind family. I could count on her mother to fix me something nice to eat and insist I stay the night. The next morning, I would hop the train and head back to Chicago.

CHAPTER EIGHT

How I Met My Wife

During this time I met my future wife, Ruth. We had a stormy relationship in the beginning. Anyone who encountered us thought we would never be married. That summer I had a job working for a steel manufacturer in Geneva. It was located right next to the Fox River by the very dam that had almost taken my life. I was living in my parents' basement which was just down the street from work.

I'll never forget our very first date. Ruthie was just a little thirteen-year-old country girl from the sleepy, small town of Virgil, when I met her. Virgil was approximately 20 miles from the Geneva and St. Charles areas.

She and her older sister Helen lived with their parents and their three younger sisters. Both girls worked as carhops at Rex's Drive-in in St. Charles, IL. I was interested in Helen.

Because I was attending art school, I asked Helen to model for me. She agreed and we scheduled a time to meet for her to view some of my previous sketches, which were all nudes. We met in a little café downtown St. Charles. Ruth arrived with her older sister but I told her I did not want her to see what I had been sketching because I knew she was too young. I realized this hurt her feelings. Helen seemed to like my artwork and we made plans for her to sit for me the following Friday night.

Later that week, Helen called to cancel our appointment because her boyfriend who worked out of town was back and of course, he wanted to spend time with her. Then, just out of the blue, she asked, "Would you like to go out with my little sister? I'll be happy to set you up with her." Just like that, I had a Friday night date.

I can still remember the night when I pulled up in their gravel driveway in my 1950 Oldsmobile. Their two-story, gray-shingle house had an attached side porch. I got out of my car and walked hesitantly up the stairs to the door. I knocked on the door and beheld the most beautiful sight stepping out onto the porch; she took my breath away.

Standing there in a yellow, checkered sundress was, in my eyes, the most beautiful girl I had ever seen. Was it love at first sight? Who can say? I can recall having the craziest thought and thinking to myself this was the girl who I wanted to have to raise my children. At that time, I never thought about marriage or family which is what made this notion so outlandish. Four-years later, she became my wife.

The first ten-years of our marriage had lots of issues and was a real rollercoaster for both of us. Having always taken care of only myself, I had become very selfish and self-centered. I was aggressive and overly dominating. The demons within me caused me to act out my most destructive and ugly tendencies. Only after I met Jesus Christ and claimed Him as my savior was I able to be delivered from so many evil things which had me bound up for so long.

Ruth is the kindest, most forgiving, amazing woman I have ever known. She has nurtured and stood alongside me through thick and thin. Ruth has never wavered in her love for me, and she is a true saint in every respect. Currently, we have been married for fifty-eight years.

What a blessing! God did choose the right mate for me.

CHAPTER NINE
SCHOOL AGAIN?

After a while, I got tired of this routine and quit art school and my job as well. I was ready to go back to high school. To my amazement, I found out the academy in Broadview, IL had been sold. It was being relocated on a five-hundred-acre parcel of land between Geneva and Elburn, IL. A whole new facility had been built, including homes for the teachers. There also was a farm on the property.

When I went back to school, I was told a funny story by one of my teachers. Seventh Day Adventists are vegetarians but for some reason the school decided to raise feeder cattle. After contacting a nearby cattle rancher, the whole faculty was invited to a big dinner. As they sat around a large table, servers walked in with beautiful platters of prime rib-eye and set one before each of them. They all gasped with horror as they looked upon this pink, rare flesh. I don't know the rest of the story; it had to be a sticky situation between honoring their own beliefs and not being rude to their hosts.

At school, I met and began dating a tall, blonde girl. One of the school rules was you were not to be alone with your girlfriend. One afternoon, I asked her if she would meet me at the farm office about a quarter mile off-campus where nobody would find us. She agreed, but to our dismay, the farm manager caught us in his office. I knew we were in real trouble.

The next day, the principal called me into his office. He asked me if I was acquainted with the school rules. I said yes. He then asked me if I would promise never to do that again. I agreed. After I left his office, I could not find my girlfriend. Someone told me she had been expelled from school. Talk about God's grace in my life. It truly was unbelievable, and I did not understand it until years later.

Another incident was when I got caught sneaking back on campus half drunk. I had a buddy from Geneva that used to come out and pick me up and we would drink together. When the dorm lights were turned off, it meant you had better be in your room or you would receive demerits. After so many demerits, you would be expelled from school.

One night after the dorm lights were off, my dean caught me stumbling up the sidewalk after being out with my friend. He asked me what was going on. He knew I was drunk. I told him I just wanted to kill myself. He took me by my arm and helped me back into the dorm. When I got to my room, he opened the door and said goodnight. I never heard another thing about it.

Another time this same dean took me up on the roof which was directly above my dorm window.

He pointed to all the empty beer cans someone had thrown about and asked me if I knew how they got there. Although, we both knew the truth of the matter, this man was so kind and forgiving toward me. The Lord placed many godly people before me during this troubling time in my life. Here again, I was shown great favor.

Once I stole some large cans of fruit from the school pantry. I planned to eat them at my leisure, so I hid them in the barn. A few days later, we had a guest speaker who taught about honesty and integrity. I immediately fell under conviction for my petty thievery and told the dean about my crime. He went with me to the barn and after viewing the cans he told me to put them back where I got them. I was never reported, nor did I receive any demerits. I know beyond a doubt God wanted me at that school, at that time in my life.

The academy had a work program, and I got a job at their factory called Harris Pine Mills. The factory had a slogan, "Do it right or not at all". This was a life lesson that I have tried to practice to this day.

My senior year, I decided to go back to school. I had skipped another year and I was going on twenty-one years of age. My mother told me I would never graduate from high school and I was determined to prove her wrong.

When I arrived at school, I was called into the principal's office. The principal suggested that I should find another school. He suggested Wisconsin Academy.

CHAPTER TEN
WISCONSIN ACADEMY

I took the advice of the staff at Broadview and enrolled in Wisconsin Academy for my senior year. I was determined to graduate high school, so my dad and Ruth drove me to the school. I buckled down that year and even made the A-B Honor Roll. This was an entirely new experience for me. I was proud to have my dad, mom and Ruth come to my graduation.

Ruth also graduated high school just a few weeks later. We spent that summer working and dating. Ruth was still car hopping at Rex's Drive-In and in the fall, she went inside as a waitress. I had a pretty good job with a construction company called Contemporary Builders and lived in an apartment in Glen Ellyn that I got rent-free because I was a custodian.

Everything was going smoothly so I decided it was time to think about getting wed. Ruth loved the idea and had wanted to be married for a long time already. We did not tell our parents about our intentions or ask for their blessing.

We decided to secretly go off and elope. Back then, a blood test was required before we could obtain the marriage license. After getting our blood drawn, we had to wait for the results to be sent to us. After about a week, we were called back to the doctor's office and required to give blood again because the first batch was contaminated as it was not properly sealed.

We planned to marry on two or three occasions, but something always came up, so it never happened. Ruth was extremely unhappy about this. One day when I stopped by her workplace, she said, "If you don't marry me now, I have someone else who surely will!" Wow! I was in shock, what a girl! There could be no more stalling so, I on the spot agreed! She said she would find someone to marry us that very night when she got off work at 11 p.m. I didn't think it would be possible but somehow, she pulled it off. Ruth was able to line up a justice of the peace and two witnesses who promised to meet us at the Municipal Building in St. Charles at midnight. I was in shock my future bride was able to arrange this on such short notice and at such a late hour.

I picked Ruth up after work and because we were about a half-hour early, we stopped for ice cream. It was a cold winter night and we were still enjoying our yummy treats when our two witnesses arrived. They were a married couple who lived on a farm not far away.

Both were dressed in dirty coveralls, big rubber boots and smelled of manure. Ruth still had on her white waitress uniform and I wore a bulky red ski sweater and blue jeans. Soon the Justice of the Peace arrived and unlocked the door.

Our witnesses followed him in and because we were still licking our ice cream cones and didn't want to waste them, we stuck them in a big snowbank near the car. Just the tips of the wooden sticks were visible.

We then rushed up to the second floor to participate in our great life-changing event. During the ceremony, I could see out of the big window next to where the Justice of the Peace sat and I detected a big boxer near our car; suddenly he began sniffing around and then he dug up our ice cream bars. He began eating them.

I nudged Ruth and as soon as she saw what was going on outside, we both burst out laughing. We laughed so hard we were in tears and just couldn't stop. Our witnesses and the Justice of the Peace acted like nothing was going on and just continued with the wedding.

Finally, he came to the part where he asked, "Do you..." We both voiced our "I Do". Still laughing, we all signed the marriage certificate and left to go our separate ways. I am sure they thought we had both been drinking! I took my new bride back to her parents' house where she continued to live for about two weeks until we figured out a way to tell them about our marriage.

This was hard on her parents because we had gone against their spiritual beliefs and it took a while for them to accept our choices. Ruth moved into my apartment in Glen Ellyn. I was still working for Contemporary Builders at that time. Later that year, we bought and moved in an old, dilapidated farmhouse in West Chicago, Illinois.

I had become disgruntled at work by the way the carpenter foreman was cheating the company. I finally told the owner what was going on. I then turned in my resignation letter and said that foreman, if not stopped, would ruin their business. Just a little while later, I heard about a shake-up at Contemporary Builders and the carpenter foreman had been fired.

The next year was rough financially and money was hard to come by. To raise cash, I built a worm farm down in our antiquated, concrete basement. Because we lived on a corner, we were able to post signs saying, "FISHING WORMS FOR SALE". People would knock on our door at all hours asking for worms. My wife's job was to go down into our dark basement and fetch, sort, and count the worms by the dozen. It was not a great money maker, but it did provide milk money for our baby girl, Carla, who was born during our first year of marriage.

I finally got a job with Combined Insurance Company out of Chicago. This kept me on the road and away from home five days a week. I was the first person who I sold a health insurance policy to and this turned out to be a wise decision.

Our old farmhouse had no insulation. We had an old fashion kitchen and cooked on a cast-iron wood-burning stove. Because we didn't have hot water, we used that little stove to heat any water we needed even our bath water which we poured into a large tin washtub we hauled into the kitchen.

We shared the water - Ruth first and then me. Later, we'd bale all the water out and drag the tub away until the next time. That cast-iron, wood-burning stove was also the only heat we had to warm the house!

In the winter, our home was exorbitantly cold and drafty. Because of this our little girl, Carla, came down with a bad, hacking cough. Her lungs were congested and she was diagnosed with pneumonia. We had to admit our tiny four-month-old baby to the hospital. Because I was on the road at this time, Ruth took the train from West Chicago to Geneva every day to visit her. Fortunately, our new insurance plan completely paid for her five-day stay.

I hated traveling and quit that job and took a position with International Harvester in Melrose Park. Our life started to improve at this point. My wife no longer had to go out at night after rain to find nightcrawlers to sell on our street corner!

We maintained and lived on a tight budget. I gave Ruth $20 a week to buy groceries for the family. Every Friday, I would allow her to buy me the ninety-nine-cent ribeye steak special. Boy, wasn't I a great guy back in those days? It was called me, me, me. I remember one time she had her $20 food allowance with her when she and Carla took a detour on the way to the grocery store and wound up at Brookfield Zoo.

Mother and daughter were laughing and having a fun time in the monkey house when Ruth realized she had been the victim of a pickpocket. Both the grocery money and car keys were gone!

Ruth was very embarrassed to call me at work and ask me to bring another set of keys. I guess I didn't get my steak that week.

I also started a lawn maintenance business. On Fridays, I worked the night shift. This allowed my wife and I to mow lawns during the day. From my paycheck at International Harvester, I was able to put $99 a week into my credit union savings account. I did this faithfully every week and our money soon began to grow.

Our transportation for our lawn business was an aged Volks-wagen Beetle that pulled a one-wheel trailer attached to the back bumper. We used it to haul our push mower and grass trimmers. Sometimes I would leave my wife and our young daughter off to mow a lawn while I went to do something else. When I returned, I could always count on her to have done a good job.

CHAPTER ELEVEN
A TRIP TO COLLEGE

After about three years, we received an offer to sell our farmhouse. As you can imagine, we jumped at this opportunity. We decided to use the money from the house sale to attend college. I definitely wasn't college material, although Ruth was. She had always been a good student and had already taken her college entrance exams. I wasn't a good student and was not prepared for higher education.

We planned to enroll in Andrews University, a Seventh Day Adventist College, located in Berrien Springs, Michigan. I guess we figured we could just show up at school and would automatically be able to attend. After my high school experiences at Broadview Academy, I wanted to become a minister and I hoped that this would be my opportunity.

Upon arrival in Michigan, we found a small apartment to rent just off-campus and within walking distance of all the academic buildings. The school year was just about to begin, and we arrived on Friday, the last day of registration. Classes were scheduled to commence on Monday.

I didn't know that I was required to take an entrance exam to be admitted. It was too late to take the exam on Friday because sunset was the beginning of their Sabbath and it continued until sunset Saturday. This day was set aside, and no one worked during this time. I told the administrator we had already moved and rented a place down the road. He said, "I will make an exception for you and I will give you the test on Sunday morning."

Bright and early Sunday morning, I walked into his office, and I was handed the test. I was escorted to a desk where I began going through the questions. I was elated to find many of the questions were multiple choice. I always was a good guesser! I finished my test in about half the allotted time. Surprisingly, later the same day, I was contacted and informed I had been accepted into the school. No one in their right mind would have ever believed I could pass that test. Here again, I found favor with the Lord.

My wife and I bought the books we needed for our first semester at their bookstore that day and we were ready for school Monday morning. It wasn't long before I began skipping classes. I also began to sneak into town to eat burgers. Many Seventh Day Adventists were vegetarian, and we also lived that lifestyle. My wife always knew when I had burgers because she could smell them on my breath. I also shot a few pigeons in the rafters of the school barn. Yum!

While at school, we decided to buy a new car. The brakes on our Volkswagen Beetle had gone bad and we were having serious motor issues. I was still carrying several thousand dollars' worth of Traveler's Checks from our house sale.

We planned to trade our old car in on a brand-new Chevy Nova. We made a trade-in deal with our car and two-thousand dollars in Traveler's Checks. Our salesman asked if he could take our Beetle for a ride. With crossed fingers, I permitted him and held my breath. In just a few minutes, he returned and pulled the car into the garage. We shook hands and the deal was done. As we were departing, I noticed he had left the car running and the garage was filling with smoke. In the nick of time for us, the deal was done, and we headed home in our brand-new car.

Because I skipped classes almost every day and had nothing going on, I decided to leave school and move back to Illinois. My wife was nearing the end of her first semester and chose to stay behind with our three-year-old daughter. Regrettably she also dropped out right before finals and hitched a ride back to Illinois with one of her girlfriends. A little later, we drove back up and retrieved our belongings.

We found an apartment in St. Charles, and I went back to work for International Harvester. Somehow, I bumped into a boyhood friend named Stanley. He had just gotten out of the Navy and needed a place to stay; we could use help with the rent so I asked if he would like to share our apartment. Without delay he said yes and moved into a large room in the back. He was able to secure a job working at the same place I did. It was very convenient, and we were often able to share rides.

After a while, I purchased a small motorcycle to use for transportation to and from work. I was always trying to save money!

One day late in the afternoon, I was riding home by myself on Route 64. Back then, a rider could lock down the handlebars with a knob when he was traveling at a high speed. I was cruising at about sixty miles per hour. In an instant, a large semi-truck pulled right out in front of me. It was way too late to unlock my handlebars. I applied my brakes and immediately went into a skid. I could not control my bike and the front end began to wobble. This is what bikers call, "the death wobble".

As the truck straightened up, my bike started to sway to the left and then to sway back to the right. My front tire slid right under the rear end of the truck and angled sideways off toward the shoulder of the road. The bike had flipped on its side and I crawled on top of it holding on as tightly as possible. I went sliding straight past the semi. Sparks were shooting everywhere and finally my bike and I came to a stop.

The trucker applied his brakes and pulled over on the shoulder just a little way from me. He jumped out of this truck and breathlessly ran toward me. He kept repeating, "Are you ok? Are you ok?" "Hell no!", I said. I bent over and picked up my bike. I swirled it around and then threw it precisely at him.

The bike hit the ground right in front of him and I began walking toward him. I pointed my finger at him and growled, "I'm going to kill you." His eyes got big as saucers as he started backpedaling. He turned and rapidly raced to his truck. In about two minutes, he was gone. That was the first and last time I ever encountered him.

Miraculously, my bike was not badly damaged and I was able to drive it home. When I picked it up off the ground, I noticed my little finger was missing the nail. I never even felt it when this happened. Other than that, I only had a couple of minor burns. I am sure, once again a supernatural power watched over me. What is that power? It is the Lord who has rescued me from death so many times throughout my life. The psalmist King David, said, "You have delivered me from death."

Later that year, we purchased and moved into a little house in Elgin, Illinois. The lady who owned the house allowed us to make monthly payments to her for three years and at the end of that time, we paid off the remainder of our debt. The total cost of that house was seven-thousand dollars.

I ran a successful lawn maintenance business out of that property. I specialized in dethatching and fertilizing lawns. I worked very fast and only did front lawns. My helper and I would first dethatch and rake off the dead grass. We would then fertilize it. As another included service, we hauled off the old grass. Our fertilizer cost us not more than three dollars per lawn and we charged a flat rate of twenty-five dollars.

Whenever we got a job in a new subdivision, it wasn't long before all the neighbors wanted their lawns done also. I often made as much as two-hundred dollars per day profit. We crammed as many giant bags of thatch into the back of our 1950 Chevy pick-up truck as possible. Our truck had a steel camper on the back of it and we piled it high with those huge, black plastic bags.

We must have looked crazy driving down the highway with bulging bags of thatch stacked sky high and tied down as not to topple off onto passing cars. When we arrived home, we dumped all this brown grass over a steep hill which ran behind and alongside our home. We felt this was a great dumping spot and it sure saved me a lot of money I would have had to pay for disposal otherwise.

I also started a spray paint business that year. I grasped how to create jobs and I could hustle to earn extra money. I purchased one of the most expensive Graco Airless Spray Guns with an additional one hundred feet of hose. With this spray gun, I could paint the inside of a new house in approximately four hours. This did not include the trim work. A realtor contacted me and wanted one of his houses painted. I told him if he supplied the paint, I would spray the entire exterior for one-hundred and twenty-five dollars. He excitedly agreed and said he would have the paint at the house by 9 a.m. the following morning. I assured him that I would have the job completed by noon the same day. He looked at me in disbelief. I told him to just wait and see and to be back at noon.

He owned a two-story house. It had a one-car garage sitting right next to it which was not part of our painting agreement. At noon when he showed up, I was sitting and relaxing on the back of my truck. I had just finished cleaning the paint sprayer. I had also painted his garage. He said this was unbelievable. He was delighted with the job and paid me without hesitation The main reason I held onto my full-time position at International Harvester was because of their excellent health benefits.

After a while, we sold our Elgin home and purchased a cottage in Barrington Hills. This was my wife's dream house. It was a quaint country home surrounded by big, oak trees and enclosed with a stylish, white picket fence. It had a large well-kept yard and a nice garage. It was exactly what Ruth had always wanted. The sale of our house in Elgin left enough money for us to pay cash for our new Barrington Hills home. We even had a little money to spare.

While working at International Harvester, I met Howard. Almost daily, whenever I ran into him, he would witness to me and give me a little Christian tract about salvation and the steps necessary to becoming a follower of Christ. Because of his faithfulness to witness to me, my wife accepted Christ after reading the literature I carried home in my pockets.

After I, too, committed my life to Christ, Howard became our spiritual parent. He introduced us to other born-again Christians, took us to Bible studies, and showed us how to become involved in street witnessing. Howard took us under his wing and taught us many things at that time in our lives.

A few months after I became a Christian, I was driving down Anderson Boulevard in Geneva, when I experienced a "divine appointment". I passed a small, white church along the road. A few cars were in the parking lot and I felt an urge to turn around and see what was going on inside. I had driven down that street many times but never noticed the little church before. It had a series of steps going up to the entrance door.

I walked inside and was warmly greeted by a woman who welcomed me and asked me my name. I introduced myself and mentioned I was a new Christian who had only a short while ago been saved. Her face lit up with excitement when I said that! "Did you say that you are Dale Kenyon?", she asked. When I nodded, she continued, "I meet you when you were in public school and always had a burden for you. All these years, I have been praying God would snag you and reel you into his kingdom!" Talk about an answered prayer!

The encounter was not meant only for me. It was God's way of showing this dear woman he was rewarding her faithfulness in prayer. She is a special saint, and I am indebted to her for her prayers and support. I hope to meet her again someday!

CHAPTER TWELVE
A SUPERNATURAL
CALL TO MISSOURI

Mere words cannot express the wonders of God! Psalms 40:5 - "Many, O Lord my God, are the wonders you have done. The things you planned for us no one can recount to you; were I to speak and tell of your deeds, they would be too many to declare."

As I look back on our move from Illinois to Missouri, I can see how God was laying out a supernatural plan for my life and for that of my family. God introduced many people into my life as we followed and obeyed him.

One day while I was working my job at International Harvester God spoke to my heart, "John, quit your job." I walked out of work that day and never looked back. I had no back-up plan and no idea of what was to come. But as I left, I knew I had walked through a giant gate to freedom. It seemed like handcuffs had fallen from my wrists. I have never forgotten the emotion of that moment or the wonderful feeling which enveloped me. What joy and what peace filled my soul!

After leaving the plant, I jumped into my truck and headed for home. I was so excited at what had just happened I could hardly wait to tell my unsuspecting wife. As I walked into our home, I saw her standing by our kitchen sink, washing dishes. She noticed me and looked straight at me as I without hesitation uttered softly, "Honey, I have just quit my job." She calmly responded, saying, "Yes, I already know . The Lord told me just a little while ago that you were going to quit." Please understand, we had never discussed this topic before.

As I walked into our living room, I was struck by the enormity of my decision. I had just given up my job and jeopardized the security of my family. I prayed, "Lord, what about my family?" He reminded me, "I'll take care of your family." I continued, "Well, what about our health insurance?" His response was, "Don't worry, I am your insurance." At that moment, I realized my heavenly Father had just made a covenant with my family. It became a covenant of blessings. God declared that this covenant would be passed on from one generation to another.

Psalms 78:4 - "We will not hide from their children, but tell to the coming generations the glorious deeds of the Lord, and His might and wonders that he has done."

As it was with Abraham, so it was with our family. He led us to our promised land here in the beautiful Lake of the Ozarks.

It has been a long and glorious adventure. After I left my job, my wife and I had no idea what we were going to do next. The area in which we lived was experiencing a spiritual revival.

We were fortunate to see many miraculous things happen as God called his people into situations they had never experienced. Many people were being saved at this time. Many others were leaving their denominational churches and becoming involved in house fellowships and street ministries.

There was an outpouring of God's Holy Spirit in the early seventies as evidenced by the speaking in tongues. The Apostle Paul wrote that many spiritual gifts existed and speaking in tongues was one of them. As new believers, my wife and I had never heard of this gift nor witnessed it.

We had an opportunity to attend a huge rally in Chicago. Charles and Frances Gardner Hunter, two legendary Christian figures at that time, were the key speakers. They were mightily ministering God's word that night. At one point in the evening, they called anyone who would like to have their marriage blessed. We found ourselves hurrying up on stage where we stood with a line of other young couples. Charles began to lay hands on and pray for each twosome individually. When our turn came, he lightly touched our foreheads as he prayed the blessing on us, and down we both fell backwards.

The next thing I remember was waking up and lying on the floor next to my wife. I heard her speaking in a strange language. New and unusual words began to flow out of my mouth also. Someone from the ministry team came to help us back up on our feet. I felt like I was drunk! A short time later, I realized that what I had experienced was a taste of new wine.

When a Christian abstains from the old wine, he can understand the uniqueness of the new wine and how it has the power to change one's life.

"But you will receive power when the Holy Spirit comes upon you." -Acts 1:8 "

But God hath revealed them unto us by His Spirit for the Spirit searches all things, yea, the deep things of God." -1 Corinthians 2:10 .

I want to share with you how quickly our enemy, Satan, can come in and refute what God has revealed to the believer. This is the same tactic he used on Eve in the Garden of Eden. If allowed, Satan will bring doubt regarding a truth God has just disclosed. Always remember that the more we follow God's leading, the clearer His instructions will become. He does have a perfect and divine plan for each one of us.

A few days after our exciting trip to Chicago, we were relaxing at home when we heard a knock at our back door. Upon opening the door, I was surprised to see a guy standing there holding a Bible in his hand. He introduced himself as a friend of someone we knew very well. Of course, we invited him in and began to visit with him. He said he belonged to a missionary training center located near where we would soon be living in Missouri. We were interested in all the things he had to say and the experiences he had as he ministered to the people he encountered.

After he finished talking, I began to share with him what had happened to us in Chicago.

He looked directly at me and said, "Speaking in tongues is from the Devil." In response I proclaimed, "That is not true." I looked it up in the Bible and discovered an exact description of what we had experienced. Things cooled off a bit after this discussion and before long, he was ready to depart.

I cordially escorted him to the door and while shaking his hand, bid him goodnight. I was not willing to engage in a theological argument with him. Even though, we were not in agreement on the baptism of the Holy Spirit, we did become good friends after our move to Missouri. Several years later, while reflecting on this incident, I realized that this had been a divine appointment.

I recall a special person God put in my life. His name was Roy and I met him while I worked at International Harvester. Roy was a CEO and somehow, we struck up a good friendship. We eventually became partners in a land transaction in Missouri. When my family moved to Missouri, we still owned two houses and a duplex in Illinois. We were in the process of selling them but did not close on any of them until after our move down south. By the time this was about to happen, Roy had left International Harvester and started a new career as a lawyer. He graciously volunteered to take care of all the paperwork relating to my property sales. He refused to take any pay for his work.

Some years later, the two of us sold our investment property. Roy told me we made four times our investment. We were both happy. That time, I insisted on taking care of the closing costs. We had so many supernatural occurrences in our lifetime.

The Lord guided us on this exciting journey and always put the right people in our pathway.

In Proverbs 3:5-6, the Bible instructs us, *"Trust in the Lord with all your heart and lean not on your own understanding; in all ways acknowledge him, and he shall direct your paths."*

I always desired to live on a lake and to become a millionaire. The millionaire part was because I wanted to show my mother, I could make something of myself and I knew she would be impressed if I had lots of money. After becoming a Christian, I never again pursued my dream for wealth. God had much greater things waiting for me.

Not sure what God wanted us to do next, we decided to take a trip to Dallas, Texas where we heard there was going to be a Christian book expo. Maybe God wanted us to open a Christian bookstore! We packed the kids, by then my son Eric was born, and headed for Dallas. We had just purchased a new Ford station wagon. As we headed down the interstate early Tuesday morning, our alternator light suddenly went on.

I pulled over to look under the hood but couldn't find anything wrong. Nothing was open in the area we were in so we pressed on to find a Ford dealership. I had two choices.

We could go to Lebanon, Missouri which was about twenty-five miles away or we could take a quite curvy and hilly road which led to Camdenton.MO.

I chose Camdenton and we arrived in town at around 5 a.m. We parked in the lot at the Ford Dealership and waited for someone to come and open for the day's business.

My wife and children were still sleeping so I decided to walk to a little coffee shop we passed as we went through the center of town. It looked like a few locals were enjoying their early morning coffee . I chose a quiet corner booth and as I sat sipping a steaming hot mug of coffee, I felt the Holy Spirit prompt me to visit a quaint stone real estate building on my way back to the car.

I assumed no one would be in at such an early hour but God was prompting me, and He always knew what was right for me. It was not a huge surprise to see one car parked in the driveway and one realtor sitting behind his desk as if waiting for me.

After introducing myself, I told him I was interested in looking at a lake home for my family. He seemed eager to accommodate me. At that time, real estate was moving very slowly in the lake area. It was a difficult business to be involved in. Jimmy Carter was our president, and our country was experiencing some financial difficulties. One issue was with our lending institutions, which were charging high interest rates on property loans.

While the realtor checked for available homes, I ran down the road to check on my family. At the car dealership, their mechanic had already looked at our car and found nothing serious was wrong. We had some type of loose connection, which he rapidly fixed and didn't even charge us for his services. We left and went back to see Don, our new real estate agent. Was the Lord setting us up for our next adventure?

Suddenly, we had no desire to continue to Dallas but understood we were here in Camdenton for a reason. Don found listings for two lake properties which sounded like good choices. The first property turned out to have already been sold and the second one did not appeal to us. Don said that was about all that was available. After getting his permission, I paged through his listing folder and found two more interesting parcels. I felt that the Lord was saying, "No" to the first place. After viewing the last spot, I believed it was the perfect site.

My wife was sitting on a stump outside of the house and the kids were playing next to her. I knew she would not be happy to hear my news. The house looked like a building that belonged on an old-time fishing camp. It was a tin structure and had no interior walls or insulation. Although it sat on a large and gorgeous lake lot, the property was covered in vines and weeds. Ruth got quiet and started to cry.

We decided to go have some lunch and take some time to pray about our decision. We would meet Don at his office later in the afternoon.

God is so wonderful, because in a short time we agreed on that rundown lake property. We made an offer of twenty thousand dollars, which is what I heard God say.

Don was disbelieving and said the owners would never take such a low offer. We were confident that this property would be ours and we signed a contract right then. When Don questioned us about the financing, I turned and said, "We will pay cash." Not many people would want to make that shabby building into their home.

It wasn't much to look at, but it did have an adequate well, outdated kitchen, and a very small bathroom with an equally small tub. To make bedrooms, we would need to hang up sheets as dividers. Under the house sat a dug-out basement with an earth floor. The reason we were familiar with Camdenton is because we had vacationed there several times in the summer. We even owned some acreage outside of town which we bought as an investment. We had a lot of acreage--six hundred and forty acres to be exact. It never occurred to us to build a house or move a trailer on this property. One of the parcels even had a spring-fed lake on it. An old-timer told me it was called "Hidden Valley Trout Farm" at one time. Nice name! I can truthfully say it was a hidden force that led our family every step of the way.

We were back home in Illinois for only a few days when we received a phone call from Don. "I can't believe it, the seller has accepted your offer and is planning a rapid closing." We now needed to sell our home in Barrington and have it listed quickly.
About six months before, a gentleman who happened to be driving by, stopped at our house one evening while my wife and I were sitting outside. He took an instant liking to our home and wanted to know if we would be interested in selling it. We took his num-

ber, saying if we ever did decide to move and sell our home, we would call him first.

The next morning our phone rang. It was the man who fell in love with our house, wanting to know if we had considered his offer to purchase our home.

I thought to myself, Wow! God really works fast. We easily agreed on a fair price. He said he had saved ten-thousand dollars cash for his down payment and he would easily be able to procure a loan for the rest. Oh, that was music to my ears!

The next morning, we went together to a local bank to apply for his loan. Everything went well and the loan officer said it would take about thirty days for everything to be approved. My buyer signed his paperwork and we left feeling like everything was in order. After thirty days had passed and we heard nothing from the loan officer or my buyer, we decided it was time to contact the bank again. What we expected to be a shoe-in turned out to be a nightmare.

Money had tightened and the banks were not making real estate loans at that time. Our buyer had been denied! What were we to do? My buyer wanted to buy our house just as much as we wanted to sell it to him.

He was determined he would find another way to finance his purchase and we were left without the money we needed to pay cash for our Missouri home.

We now needed to secure a loan for our investment. My wife and I decided to visit First National Bank in Geneva. We hoped to find favor with them. It was my parents' hometown bank and as a youth, I had an account also. My dad was friends with the loan officer, John. He was a nice guy who in later years became vice president of that bank.

 John invited us into his office, and we told him the situation we found ourselves in and how we needed to borrow twenty-thousand dollars, which was the purchase price of our new home.

He said he was so sorry but in the current economy such a loan was not possible. "Maybe", he said, "in a month or two, money may loosen up and we could talk about it then." I explained we didn't have a month or two, but needed the money now, In addition to needing the cash for our purchase, we also needed to get to Missouri and enroll our children in school by September 1st. We left the bank, knowing things were not going well for us. We decided to trust God and move anyway.

We rented a big U-Haul and with the help of some of our Christian friends, we loaded up all our belongings. My friend, Howard, volunteered to drive the truck that was filled to the brim with all our earthly possessions. He took off early in the morning because it was about an eight-hour drive and he couldn't go to fast with the big load he was carrying.

My family planned to stop off to say goodbye to my mom and dad and then meet Howard down in Camdenton. Before Howard left, he asked what he should do with the U-Haul and all our possessions if we didn't arrive in Missouri that evening or if we didn't have the money to close on our property. I was so confident God would provide for us somehow that I replied, "Just unload it all right in the center of the road, and then bring the U-Haul back home." He looked at me and questioned, "Are you kidding me?" I explained, "No, there is no way I can control what happens. I can't contact you once you leave."

Remember, back in those days we didn't have cell phones. After Howard left, we went to Geneva to have farewell breakfast with my mom and dad. My dad casually asked if we had received our loan yet. I told him, "No" and that we were leaving with only seven-hundred dollars cash on us. At that moment, I had no idea by the time we would reach Missouri, we would have in our possession the sum of twenty-thousand and seven-hundred dollars!

After we all said our good-byes and were preparing to leave, my dad said, "Let's stop by the bank before you head south." I explained to him exactly what John had proclaimed and how tight money was. But my dad insisted we stop by one last time anyway. And so once again, we found ourselves back at the bank and in John's office. John repeated all the things he had told me on my last visit.

My dad sat patiently next to me and listened to every word John voiced. Then he stood up and calmly inquired, "John, does my signature mean anything at this bank?" "Why, yes sir it does," John said.

"Then write my son a check for twenty-thousand dollars right now. He needs to be on his way." Dad commanded. I never saw a banker move faster! In less than fifteen minutes, we were presented with our much-needed funds and my family was in the car and headed south to purchase our new home. During our drive, God spoke to my heart and showed me the beautiful parallel between the power of my earthly father's signature and the enormity of using the name of our Lord, Jesus Christ. Our Father in heaven loves us so much more than we can comprehend and desires to fulfill our every need.

Matthew 7:7 - "Ask and it will be given to you; seek and you will find; knock and the door will be opened to you."

Time seemed to fly by and before we knew it, we were in Camdenton, Missouri, signing the papers necessary to acquire our new home. Everything went like clockwork. We met Howard just in time and drove to our new place to unload our possessions. In the morning, Howard headed back to Illinois.

Another friend, a Baptist minister who drove one of our cars loaded with personal items and clothing, left to go to his home in Algonquin at the same time. We told him not to ride back with Howard but instead to drive our nine-passenger Ford station wagon home because we wanted to bless him by giving it to him as a gift for his ministry. Later I visited with this friend at his home in Illinois. He told me he had put over one-hundred thousand miles on that vehicle and he was still driving it. Wow! What a God we serve!

Eventually, Howard and I lost track of each other. I was saddened when I heard he had passed away from mesothelioma, a lung cancer caused by exposure to asbestos. Even in his darkest hours, I was told he never stopped witnessing for Christ. I hope to meet him again in eternity and spend some time in his presence.

CHAPTER THIRTEEN
MISSOURI LIFE

Just a few days after our move, we enrolled our kids in school, got our house organized and began our life in the country. The season was changing, and fall was coming on. The leaves were beginning to turn bright shades of yellow and crimson red, and evenings were chilly. We were thankful we had a fireplace in the house to ward off the cold weather which was coming.

One day when I stopped in to see Don at his office, he invited me to his trailer where I met his wife, Terry and their two children. He confided to me that he had not sold any property in a long while and he had almost no food for his family. I had very little myself but enough to buy a few loaves of bread and some peanut butter for his girls.

I asked him if he would be interested in helping me cut firewood which we could sell to make some extra money. He readily agreed and that was the start of our winter project.

One crisp afternoon, after we had cut a load of wood, Don confided, "John, I am a Christian. I just recently asked Jesus to come into my heart." "Every time you said God told you something it always happened.

I couldn't help but believe there is a living God and I desire to serve him, too." Don and I spent that winter together cutting firewood, splitting rails, and praising God. In the spring, Don and his family moved to Kansas City. After a while, he sent me a letter along with a one-hundred dollar check. He said God had blessed him with over a million dollars in sales that year. This was the last time I heard from him, but I perceived his life was on track and going well.

Although I wasn't very obedient to my parents, I have learned and understand how to be obedient to God and to hear His voice. One day I decided a regular job would be good. I prayed about it and sensed the Lord reply, "yes". So, I went after a job.

I had been a welder at International Harvester in Illinois so it seemed like a welding job would be the best option. The first place I went to was a boat trailer manufacturing company. While still in the parking lot, I asked the Lord how much they were paying welders. He said, "$2.50 per hour." I went inside and inquired of the owner if they had any job openings and what their hourly rate was. "Sure we have a job for you and we are paying $2.50 per hour." That was exactly what the Lord had told me. I said, "No thanks," and got in my truck and headed to another welding shop.

The next day I started to work for Dial's Welding at $3.50 per hour. After working for a month, I noticed a disturbing pattern.

Each pay check seemed to go through my fingers like water. I asked the Lord what was going on and why I wasn't blessed or prospering. He said, "You told me that you wanted this job. If you step out in faith, I will again begin to bless you and your family." The following day I told my boss I was leaving. Although he didn't understand God's purpose in my life, he wished me well. The day after leaving my job, God blessed me with a $400 check in the mail. From that day forward God has always abundantly blessed us. We never missed a payment or lacked any necessities. *2 Corinthians 9:8 - "And God is able to bless you abundantly, so that in all things at all times, having all that you need, you will abound in every good work.*

I met a man named Earl Weisman who one day showed me a closet full of Indian and Mexican sterling silver jewelry, which he had from the days gone by when he owned a gift shop at Bagnell Dam in Lake Ozark, Missouri. He told me to take it all and sell it, and to pay him whatever I felt was fair. We split the profit and were both surprised by its popularity.

It was during this time that I began stringing turquoise nugget necklaces. I sat at the kitchen table and could work through the night stringing about one-hundred of them. I packed them in an old wooden cigar box and took them to Bagnell Dam. At the Dam, I could peddle them to the souvenir shops. I sold them for a dollar apiece and always returned home with an empty cigar box.

I was an entrepreneur in my day. My wife and I started our business with little money. The Lord blessed us by sending people into our lives at exactly the right moment.

Proverbs 16:9 - "In their hearts humans play their course, but the Lord establishes their steps."

One person who particularly stands out was Walt Tietmeyer. He was the owner of Dog-Patch, a complex of thirteen stores located in Lake Ozark, Missouri. I was introduced to Walt by his son who was a friend of mine. It as a miracle that he allowed us to lease a small cubicle in the old Dog Patch General Store which was a major shop on the strip. Walt was always gracious to our family and I grew to love him like a father. I so appreciate the opportunity he gave us, to set up our jewelry cases right in front of a large, open door leading out into the street. People walking past could look in and see our jewelry.

Our family leased a spot in the General Store for ten-years selling Indian jewelry and Arkansas diamonds. The Lord greatly blessed our business and we started going on buying trips to replenish inventory.

While on a buying trip to Albuquerque, New Mexico, I met Ralph Kalifono. He said that he was a Palestinian and that years prior, his father came to the United States and sold Indian rugs. Ralph followed in his father's entrepreneurship and founded an American

Native Indian jewelry wholesale business. He became one of our main suppliers. He trusted us and on several occasions, when we were short on funds, he would say, "Just take what you need and pay me when you make the money."

 I remember once when I was in town, I stopped and told Ralph that the Lord had shown me the price of silver was going to go up. When he asked me how high, I guessed, "Maybe to $10 an ounce." It actually escalated to $50 an ounce.

Some months later, I traveled to Mesa, Arizona where I met with a gentleman who manufactured belt buckles. I visited his plant where he was producing a special buckle order for me. The price of silver was high back then, about $40 an ounce. My friend had developed an alternative metal that was much cheaper. His product resembled silver and his buckles were exceptionally attractive. I suggested he call his new creation "Silvertine" because it only had a small amount of silver. He was excited about the new name.

 After procuring my order, I decided to visit a friend in Carlsford, New Mexico. I began on Highway 10, heading east. For some reason, instead of continuing on Hwy 10, I turned on 25 North. I said, "Lord, I don't want to go North, but I felt compelled to do so. After a while, I found myself back in Albuquerque to see Ralph.

 I was unaware that God had given me a prophetic message for Ralph. I walked into his shop where I found his brother, Bob, standing next to a huge pile of silver coins. Bob told me that Ralph was available and pointed to a large door, saying, Ralph is in that room. "Go on in", he said. What I saw when I stepped through that door was unbelievable.

There, stood Ralph and about ten other gentlemen, all gathered around a circular table that held a huge amount of money in the center. As I approached the table, I could see all the denominations of money, including one-hundred-dollar bills. Ralph glanced up and was visibly shocked to see me. He rushed to my side where he put his arm around my shoulder and began backing me out of the room. His friends seemed upset by my presence but Ralph assured them that I meant no harm. He said, "Don't worry, he's a priest.

The reason he referred to me as a priest was that I shared the story about the Lord with him. We then entered Ralphs office where he explained that some of the Palestiniar brothers love to gamble, but when the game is over, we give all the money back. Ralph certainly had a great sense of humor!

Sitting in his office, I began to share that the Lord told me the price of silver was breaking and going much lower. Little Joe, one of Ralphs brothers, who was listening to the conversation, abruptly left the room. About twenty minutes later, Joe reappeared and said, "John, you are mistaken. I just called Hong Kong, and the price of silver is still going up". Joe did not understand that I was speaking about a future event. Just a few months later, the value of silver dropped radically. Unfortunately, Ralph and his siblings took a large hit. Ralph decided to go back to his country for a while. Many years later, I met his grown son, Alex, who is an entrepreneur like his father.

He has created a fantastic business in Las Vegas, Nevada. As soon as I met Alex, we had an immediate connection just like I did with his father. I had the pleasure of reconnecting with Ralph a few years ago while on a buying trip to Las Vegas. It was great to see him again.

CHAPTER FOURTEEN
LIVES LOST

One day while filling our gas tank at our local filling station, Ruth and I met a young lady named Debbie. She worked with New Tribes, which was a language school for missionaries going overseas. The woman noticed the Bible lying in the back window of our car. She came over to our vehicle and introduced herself. We became instant friends, united in our love of Jesus. In addition to her studies at New Tribes, Debbie led a weekly Bible study for some young, incarcerated women at a prison in Jefferson City.

It was during one of the studies she met and began mentoring Sue, who was a young mother with a troubled history. In spring, Debbie graduated from school at the same time Sue was released from prison. Because Debbie was free until fall when she would go overseas and Sue had no one willing to take her in, we invited them to spend the summer at our lake house.

To be conveniently located near our shop during tourist season , we always stayed in a small cabin on the Bagnell Dam Strip.

The girls loved their time at our house and Debbie was eager to spend time ministering to Sue, hopeful to lead her to the Lord and to prepare her for her new life and the possibility of regaining custody of her son. And so it was for all of us that summer. The Lord had orchestrated his plan for our lives. It was like nothing we could have imagined.

Debbie and Sue happily settled into life on the lake, enjoying all the fun that summer in the Ozarks brings. We were situated on the Bagnell Dam strip and having a profitable selling season with the many visiting tourists.

One day, I got a curious call from Debbie. She asked if I thought a person could have a demon. I said absolutely. Debbie remarked she had been ministering to Sue for over a year and that every time she presented the salvation message to Sue and asked if she would like to accept Christ, Sue would say she was unable to comprehend what Debbie meant. She was also literally unable to utter the name, Jesus.

After hearing this story, I set up a time for the girls to come for prayer and ministry. When the ladies arrived, we prayed for God's guidance and wisdom. When I looked into Sue's eyes, I gazed upon a demon of doubt and commanded it in the name of Jesus to leave her. Sue was immediately set free.

She was overcome with joy and without hesitation, adoringly said the name, Jesus. We all three began to weep and praise the Lord. At that moment, we were experiencing Sue's rebirth into the kingdom of God.

The remaining summer, Sue blossomed and grew by leaps and bounds in her understanding and knowledge of spiritual truths.

As fall approached, Debbie made a difficult and heart-wrenching decision. Rather than leave for the mission field, she would remain behind and continue to live with and minister to Sue. They moved to Kansas City, where they rented an apartment and found jobs.

After just a few months, on October twentieth of that year, God called them both home when they were involved in a horrific car accident. God cares for those who trust in him. He has a perfect plan for our lives. God knew Debbie, whose dream was to be a missionary and to minister to many, would instead lay down her life for just one precious soul. How magnificent will be her reward in heaven!

Matthew 7:16-20 declares, "You shall know them by their fruits. Do men gather grapes from thorn bushes or figs from thistles? Even so, every good tree bears good fruit, but a bad tree bears bad fruit. A good tree cannot bear bad fruit, nor can a bad tree bear good fruit. Every tree that does not bear fruit is cut down and thrown into the fire. Therefore, by their fruits, you will know them."

I would like to relate a very different sort of encounter that also occurred at Bagnell Dam. I was sitting in a little snack bar behind Dogpatch, a complex of souvenir stores, one summer afternoon when a gentleman who was employed as a handyman for the family who owned Dogpatch walked by. I had shared the gospel of Jesus with him on several occasions.

It was obvious to me he had been drinking, which was his daily habit. He was cursing and ranting on about his best friend who he was accusing of having an illicit affair with his wife.

I knew both men and understood they were not only drinking buddies but hotheads as well. This handyman told me that he had brutally beaten up his former friend, but now was going back to rough him up some more. I warned him not to go back to that's man's house, but he was in a rage and could not be stopped. As he began to leave, he turned to me and quoted an Old Testament scripture. He said, "I believe in the Bible, an eye for an eye and a tooth for a tooth".

Within one-hour, things turned bad and one man lay dead, killed by the hands of the other. The adulterous friend lay wait at his home, fearing the handyman would return to inflict more pain. He had a loaded twelve-gauge shotgun, just in case. Even the deterrent of a loaded shotgun pointed directly at him did not stop the handyman, who charged right in and grabbed the gun barrel.

The gun was discharged, and a life was ended.

The handyman left this earth refusing to receive Christ, without hope of seeing heaven, only looking forward to eternal damnation.

Once in a vision, I was taken to the rim of hell. Looking down into that black hole, I could hear voices crying, "Lord, Lord, save us from this terrible place." I did not hear even one voice cursing or blaspheming God. Without the Lord, there is no hope!

Jesus tells a story about hell in Luke 16:19-31.

"There was a rich man who was dressed in purple and fine linen and lived in luxury every day. At his gate was laid a beggar named Lazarus, covered with sores and longing to eat what fell from the rich man's table. Even the dogs came and licked his sores.

"The time came when the beggar died and the angels carried him to Abraham's side. The rich man also died and was buried. In Hades, where he was in torment, he looked up and saw Abraham far away, with Lazarus by his side. So he called to him, 'Father Abraham, have pity on me and send Lazarus to dip the tip of his finger in water and cool my tongue, because I am in agony in this fire.'

"But Abraham replied, 'Son, remember that in your lifetime you received your good things, while Lazarus received bad things, but now he is comforted here and you are in agony. And besides all this, between us and you a great chasm has been set in place, so that those who want to go from here to you cannot, nor can anyone cross over from there to us.'

"He answered, 'Then I beg you, father, send Lazarus to my family, for I have five brothers. Let him warn them, so that they will not also come to this place of torment.'

"Abraham replied, 'They have Moses and the Prophets; let them listen to them.'

"'No, father Abraham,' he said, 'but if someone from the dead goes to them, they will repent.'

"He said to him, 'If they do not listen to Moses and the Prophets, they will not be convinced even if someone rises from the dead.'" -- Luke 16:19-31

CHAPTER FIFTEEN
WITNESSING TO THE DYING

I am so honored God has allowed me to be at the bedside of many who were at the point of death. He has allowed me to minister salvation to some of them.

I remember one time a woman came into our shop at Bagnell Dam and bought some turquoise jewelry from us. Because of one of our discussions, she recognized I was a Christian. She told me that she was very distressed because her husband was dying of cancer in the hospital at their hometown in Illinois.

She wanted me to go to the hospital and pray for him. I accepted her invitation and a couple days later, I found myself at his hospital room. I realized that he was in a coma as I sat alongside his bed and began to pray. To my surprise, I looked up, and in a vision, I saw his spirit leaving his body. God was revealing a future event to me. The next day, his wife called my home and asked me if her husband was going to recover. She was, of course, hoping that the Lord was going to heal him. I told her what I had seen. What more could I say?

Just a few days later, he passed away. As for God's believers, precious in the eyes of Jesus is the death of his beloved ones.

I was privileged to be with my brother-in-law, Jack, in his final hours. Over the years, I had shared with him his need to receive Jesus as his savior, but he never seemed to be much interested in what I had to say. One day, Jack complained to my sister Kay, that he had an extremely bad headache. After he went to the doctor, he was told to go home and take aspirin. His headache was more serious than the doctor realized or even that the hospital staff discerned after he was admitted to the emergency room.

A short time later, he was taken to a hospital in Columbia by helicopter. By the time he arrived, he was in a coma and suffering from meningitis. My sister was seated by his bedside, as I entered his room and took hold of his motionless hand. "Jack, if you can hear me, squeeze my hand." I felt his hand move in mine. " "I am here to share Jesus with you. Would you like to receive him as your savior? If so, just squeeze my hand again." Once again, I felt a small squeeze. I was taken back by the next thing that came out of my mouth. I heard myself say, "Jack, I forgive you your sins." I thought, "What am I doing? I can't forgive sins."

That evening, God showed me the scripture in 2 Corinthians 5:20 which says, "*If you forgive anyone's sins, their sins are forgiven; if you don't forgive them, they are not forgiven. Therefore, we are ambassadors for Christ, as though God were making his appeal through us.*"Here we find ourselves representing Christ on earth. Next, I said, "Jack, I am going to baptize you." I looked around for some water but none was in sight, his drinking glass was empty. I did what I could. I frantically spit on my hand and placed it on his forehead, "Jack, I baptize you in the name of Jesus". My sister, Kay, had left the room when I arrived and now came back in. When I told her what had just happened, we both began to rejoice. It wasn't long until Jack passed out of this world. I hope to see him in heaven someday.

Another time, I was visiting a sister in the Lord who had a stroke. She was already unconscious when I entered her room. No other visitors were present but I noticed her left foot was uncovered. I walked over and took hold of her big toe and I said to her, "I know that you can hear me.

" *In scripture, Jesus told the story about raising a man from the dead. It was the dead man who heard the Lord's command, "Lazarus, come out."* John11:43.

I knew this woman was able to hear my words and I assured her saying, "I am here to tell you that everything is going to be alright." After speaking these words, I went into a vision. She was standing in the center of a beautiful white arched bridge. I realized that she was about to walk over it to be in the presence of her savior. She was on her way to paradise. I can only surmise how gorgeous heaven would be for her. She went home to be with the Lord just a few days later.

These things I have seen and experienced are not unique only to me but are available to any of God's children who have the faith to believe.

God showed me an amazing thing regarding the loss of our dear family pet. I had a vision about our loving dog, Buddy.

Buddy had suffered from diabetes for over three years, taking insulin shots twice daily. Regrettably, the day came when it was time to put him down. With a heavy heart, I drove him to the animal hospital that morning. A kindly lady took him from my arms and laid him on the floor. She gently stroked him as the needle was inserted into his paw and the process began. He almost instantaneously dropped his head on his remaining front paw, and he was gone.

With tears in my eyes, I looked up and saw Jesus. So tenderly he reached down and picked Buddy up, saying, "Don't be afraid. You're home now." I hope to see Buddy again. Who knows the things that God has prepared for those who love Him? I find hope and comfort in Ecclesiastes 3:21 which states, "*who knows if the spirit of a man rises upward and if the spirit of the animal goes down into the earth.*"

I'd like to tell you about my brother-in-law, Jim Lewis. I will never forget and always be grateful for the great honor God gave me in Jim's life. For many years, I had a strong desire to share the salvation message of hope with this man.

Some people live their entire life without understanding their purpose or why God created them. All of us were created to fulfill God's eternal plan.

I still remember the day we received a phone call from my sister-in-law, Anita, who lived in Illinois. She told us her husband, Jim, who spent much of his time caring for the family farm in Arkansas, was gravely ill and had been transported by helicopter to Mercy Hospital in Springfield, Missouri, possibly suffering from a stroke. We lived only an hour and a half away so we left without delay for the hospital since it would take Anita and her daughter, Rebecca, about nine hours to drive that distance. After we drove to Springfield and located Jim's hospital room, we were surprised to see him sitting up in bed, a little dazed but alert.

We sat with him for a time awaiting Anita's arrival. After Anita arrived, a conference was convened with the doctors, who confirmed Jim had suffered a stroke but also that he had much more serious problems than we had ever suspected. The doctor was brutally frank but honest as he presented a notably negative prognosis. Jim was diagnosed with lung and brain cancer, both of which were terminal. He was given only a short time to live. We were all in shock! Ruth and Rebecca left the room to spend some time downstairs in the lounge and not to cry in front of Jim.

Anita, Jim, and I collected our thoughts and talked about the future. Jim said he was in no pain and felt fair. I took the opportunity to speak to him about his eternal salvation in Christ. When I asked him if he would like to receive Jesus, without hesitation he replied, "Yes". We then bowed our heads and prayed the salvation prayer together. Jim asked the Lord to forgive him of all his sins.

God then did a miraculous thing. God showed me that there was something in my brother-in-law that had him bound up. Two demons needed to come out of him. The first was a demon of nicotine and the second was a demon of alcohol. Jim agreed with me as I called those evil spirits out of him in the name of Jesus. They had to leave, and Jim was at once set free. A glass of water was sitting on Jim's nightstand. I used a little water from it and baptized him in the name of Jesus. While Jim was resting, I took a little break and walked downstairs to the cafeteria for a snack.

As I was sitting there, I heard God's voice say to me, "John, I have made you for this day." What a glorious revelation! God had created me for this moment in time.

The Bible declare in Ecclesiastes 3:11, "yet he has made everything beautiful in its time. He had also set eternity in the human heart, yet no one can fathom what God has done from beginning to end."

When Jim was released from the hospital, he and Anita went back to Arkansas to check on the farm. After a few days, they headed back to Illinois. Anita noticed Jim was not smoking on that long trip home, which had been his habit for years. When questioned, he just said that he had quit. Jesus was his deliverer! After arriving home, some of their friends had a little get-together for them. One of the first things a friend did was to offer Jim a beer.

He proudly replied, "No, thanks; I don't drink anymore." What an amazing God we serve. He is our redeemer! This was Jim's time and now he is home for all eternity. I will see him again when I, too, pass into the heavens to meet my Lord. What a glorious time that will be!

CHAPTER SIXTEEN
SATAN AND DEMONS

We were blessed by all the opportunities we had to minister from our Missouri home. I also had a friend who was a Methodist minister in Camdenton. We met weekly to fellowship and pray together at his church. Once, we discussed demons and the devil. He shocked me when he said, "I simply cannot believe in the existence of the devil." I replied, "One day, God is going to reveal to you the reality of the devil's existence and that he has hordes of demons."

We left it at that, but it didn't take long for him to have a powerful experience in the supernatural. It was about a week later when I got a frantic call from my pastor friend with this story. An older lady who lived across the street from his church phoned him saying that she had demons flying around her living room. "Would he please come over and get rid of them?", she exclaimed. He told me he immediately hurried across the street to see what was going on.

Upon entering the home, he could not comprehend what was occurring. Demons were flying back and forth in her living room. The woman pleaded with him to help her. He was mortified and didn't know what to say. All he could come up with was that he would pray about it and abruptly left. "I absolutely must say I will never again doubt there is a devil." he told me.

As time went on, we had many discussions and many theological differences. It seemed like we were at an impasse on numerous topics. One day as I prayed about our situation, God gave me an interesting vision. I saw a trench between the pastor's house and his church. The pastor and I kept walking back and forth in this trench. We would stop and turn when we came to the end of the furrow and then do it all over again. Every time this happened, the rut got just a little bit deeper. I could see we were getting nowhere. When this vision ended, I knew that God was saying it was time to move on. We remain friends to this day. I still love him very much and think of him often.

One day, Ruth and I met some folks while we were out and about. As we talked with them, they told us that they had a home fellowship and invited us to attend. From the first time we went, we felt welcome and hit it off with the other Christians who were meeting in this home. They were all young people like us who wanted more of Jesus in their lives. I met a lady who became a close friend of our family over time.

One day, she told me when we first met, she for some unknown reason, disliked me, almost hated me.

I think it was because I had become involved in deliverance ministry. Sometime later in one our meetings, she was delivered from a spirit of hatred. Many times, I have seen the world of spirits that are hidden from our view. The antidote for these demonic spirits is the precious blood of Jesus. By his death and resurrection, we are delivered from this present evil.

Revelation 12:11 - *"They triumphed over him by the blood of the Lamb and by the word of their testimony; they did not love their lives so much as to shrink from death."*

John 17:15 - *"My prayer is not that you take them out of the world but that you protect them from the evil one."*

Another experience I had at this same fellowship was when we were delivering one of the brothers who had an extremely powerful demon. There were times when we were calling out a demon in a particular person and demons would begin to manifest in someone else. The owner of this house recognized he had a demon and asked if we would minister to him later. We scheduled a time for a few brothers and myself to privately return to his home.

Our friend was waiting in his bedroom when we entered. We prayed a deliverance prayer together and while standing squarely in front of him, I commanded the demon to speak its name. Jesus gave us believers the power and authority to cast out demons. There is a biblical example of a time when Jesus spoke to the demon that lived in a man who Jesus approached in a cemetery.

When Jesus asked the demon his name, he replied,

"My name is Legion, for we are many." - Mark 5:9 Jesus said,

And these signs shall follow them that believe; In my name shall they cast out demons..." - Mark 16:17.

Our authority is enacted through our faith.

As I stood before my friend, his face began distorting. His tongue shot out of his mouth and forked like that of a snake. I could feel his hot breath almost like but not quite as hot as a blowtorch. I backed up a little but still stood my ground. When I commanded the demon to tell me his name, he hissed, "My name is Satan." I believe the demon was trying to scare me but it didn't work. I firmly commanded him to leave but he was defiant and refused to obey. I asked the Holy Spirit to show me what was hindering this deliverance.

We took a little break and I walked into a guest room to pray. Sitting on the dresser was a small idol carved from granite. I showed it to my friend who confirmed that it was his, but he hadn't realized it was an image of a god. Many times, demons are connected to these types of images. My friend said that he would break it up with a hammer and then dispose of it in the trash. It was getting late, so we decided to continue with the deliverance the next morning.

After we arrived the following day, something still wasn't right. Although the homeowner assured us, he had discarded the idol, we still had a hindrance with his deliverance.

I walked away for a time and into to a room where I was led directly to discover the idol hidden in a drawer.

Our friend was embarrassed to say he decided to keep the figure, thinking it was alright as long as he did not display it. After he took it outside and destroyed it, he instantly received his deliverance.

CHAPTER SEVENTEEN
ENCOUNTERING
THE SUPERNATURAL
THROUGH VISIONS

Many of my supernatural experiences with God have come by the way of visions. Some visions were daytime visions, which are a quick glimpse of what is going on in the unseen realm. One of the first visions of this type occurred after our family returned home from summer vacation.

As we pulled into the driveway, the little neighbor girl who had been watching our family dog, frantically ran up to our car. Through her tears, she told us our miniature, black dachshund, Peanuts, was very sick. She said the dog became ill after drinking out of a small plastic swimming pool we had in our back yard. He was nauseous and vomiting. Before we left for our vacation, I threw some poison into the pool to kill mosquito larva. It never occurred to me our dog would wander into the pool or that he would drink the poison.

We picked the little dog up and rushed him to our local veterinarian office which was close by. Just before I got into the car, I had a day-vision of our dog standing in our back yard, wagging his tail. At the time, I had no idea what the vision was all about. I soon understood God was conveying a message to me regarding what was about to take place.

Our vet carefully placed the sick pup on the examining table. After looking him over carefully, he shook his head and said, "This dog will not live through the night. He has obviously been poisoned." I did not clearly understand the day-vision so I replied, "That's not true because I saw my dog wagging his tail in our back yard. I know he will recover and live through this because God showed it to me."

As I spoke these words, our unbelieving veterinarian began to roll his eyes and look at my wife. He seemed to be signaling that maybe I was a little crazy. He told us if our dog survived, we should bring him back in three days and he would take another look at him. I'm sure he probably thought he would never see us again.

Three days later, we showed up at the veterinarian's office with our dog. After examining Peanuts again, he turned to us and exclaimed in disbelief, "This is not the dog I examined three days ago."

We assured him that it was the same dog, healed by God, and we reminded him of the vision I had. The veterinarian was amazed. He exclaimed, "This truly is a miracle!" I said, "We have experienced so many miracles so we plan to write a book about them in the future." The veterinarian told he would be glad to write a letter of confirmation, explaining that this definitely was a miracle.

On a trip back to Illinois I was witnessing to a woman who was not a Christian. Her adult children had been faithfully praying for her salvation for years. While chatting with her, I received a vision of multiple clay tablets laying at the feet of Jesus, he told me that one of these tablets was the prayers of her children. He said today he was going to honor their prayers.

I asked the woman if she knew what was going to happen when she died. She said she did not know. I explained the salvation of Jesus and she accepted Christ as her savior that day.

The next vision I experienced was while I was standing on a large, flat rock behind our home, which overlooked Lake of the Ozarks in central Missouri.

Looking over the lake in the distance, an arched bridge appeared before me. Someone appeared on the other side of the bridge waving at me and beckoning me to cross over. I realized it was Jesus who was calling to me. Stepping out onto the bridge, I saw a huge, jagged pile of junk right in the middle and I was unable to climb it. "Lord," I cried out, "I cannot come to you."

At that point, the vision ended and it was not until years later I was able to understand what the Lord was conveying to me. I couldn't comprehend the significance of that junk piled high in the middle of the bridge until much later in my life.

God reminded me of an occurrence that took place when I was five-years old. I had a strange encounter with a demonic spirit. It happened one afternoon as I was about to take a nap in my parents' bedroom.

As I lay on their bed, I experienced a presence which took hold of me and caused me to react in a most bizarre fashion.

To this day, I clearly remember that incident. I couldn't under-stand what was going on at that time, but years later after I became a Christian, the Holy Spirit revealed to me through another vision that I previously received an evil spirit.

A person does not have to be involved in gross sin for these vicious demons to attack. They will use any opportunity they can to invade someone's body. They try to hide and use any means not to be discovered. That body becomes the demon's residence. After attaining residence, these vile spirits will often invite other demons to dwell with them.

Mark 5:9 - "Then Jesus asked him, "What is your name?" "My name is Legion," he replied, "For we are many." 1 Corinthians 3:16 - "Do you know that you yourselves are God's temple, and now the Spirit of God dwells in your?"

Jesus tells the story about going into the temple of God and casting out all of those who sold their goods there.

He declared to them, *"My temple will be called a house of prayer, but you have turned it into a den of thieves." - Matthew 21:13.*

You may be wondering why I am sharing these things, and it is because they are some of my personal experiences.

My body was invaded by these ungodly merchants and money-changers.

Today, these entities are called demons. They can and will invade both Christians and non-believers when given the opportunity. In one of my visions, I saw two demons departing my body out through the top of my head. Was the Spirit of God in my body which is God's temple? Of course, he was. His abode is in the Holy of Holies, which is in every Christian.

A vision is one way of pulling back the curtain in the spiritual realm and letting one see that which he is dealing with. I would like to share a vision I had at our home.

It was a Saturday night and we had invited some friends over for a Bible study and prayer meeting. I was sitting on our couch when suddenly, I saw the roof of our house open up. As I looked up through the opening where the roof used to be, I saw an army of angels standing side-by-side up on the hillside.

Psalms 91:11 - "For he will command his angels concerning you to guard you in all your ways."

I began to describe to the group what I was seeing and said angels were all around our home. One lady asked me what the angels looked like. I could only portray them as having bright, bronze faces and long, white robes.

This vision was a warning that our adversary, the devil, was going to attempt to harm our family.

Sometimes a vision can seem mystifying until it becomes a reality. I did not take long before the context of this vision came to pass. One early morning, two-weeks later, my wife got up to use the bathroom which was situated on the other end of our home. When she flushed the toilet, steam came billowing out of it, accompanied by a large explosion.

I was awoken by the blast, but before I could even get past our kitchen the whole house was full of hot vapor. I had to crawl across the kitchen floor on my hands and knees.

When I got to the bathroom, the steam had already dissipated. The lid had blown off the water tank on the back of the toilet and lay cracked on the floor before me. When I looked down into the tank, I saw the insides had completely melted. I double-timed it outside to where our water tank and wellhead were and opened the lid to look inside. The tank itself was too hot to touch. The hot water heater was positioned in our basement directly under our bathroom floor and right next to our children's bedroom.

I can only imagine what would have happened to our family if that hot water tank had exploded. My wife was prompted to flush the toilet at exactly the right time. I know that was not a coincidence. Once again, God was looking out for us.

One evening while I was driving home from a Bible study, I began to worship God and to inquire of Him what He wanted for my life. At that time, we were being greatly blessed through a business He had developed for us. As I was speaking to the Lord, I declared, "Lord, I will follow you wherever you want me to go. I will move; I will throw my business in a garbage can if you want. I will do anything for you." His word came strongly back to me and I will never forget it. His response was, "Are you willing to suffer the consequences of following me?" Without thought or hesitation, I replied, "Yes, Lord."

At that particular time in our lives, God had opened a door for us to sell Indian Jewelry. We had many opportunities to minister to the people we met in our business and God financially blessed us.

We were able to finish remodeling our lake house and to pay cash for all the improvements we made.

c

Our new business prospered and only required us to work about five months out of the year. In the wintertime when we weren't working, we stored our jewelry in a large wooden box we kept on the concrete floor of our bedroom closet. One evening as I pulled down our driveway and stepped out of my truck, I had a vision of a large fire ablaze in our kitchen. Flames were leaping everywhere. I asked the Lord what I was seeing and He plainly said, "In the morning, call your insurance agent."

Because we had just recently finished building and remodeling our home, we had not yet increased our homeowner's insurance. I called our insurance provider and instructed him to update our insurance coverage. After viewing our home, it took him just a few days to make everything current.

About six months later, our home was destroyed in a fire. We lost everything we owned, including our jewelry business. Incidentally, our jewelry inventory was composed mostly of sterling silver. All of it melted into our concrete floor. Later, I scooped it all up and put it into a small garbage can that was sitting nearby. Our inventory of about $35,000 of silver jewelry was not covered by insurance, but our home was completely insured thanks to God's prompting.

I don't know how the garbage can got on our property or into our burned-out bedroom. Some years later, I told the story to one of our jewelry salesmen.

He asked if I still had that garbage can with the melted silver and if I would be willing to part with it. He offered me a fair sum of money and I was happy to sell it to him. Thinking back to our house fire, the morning after the fire, the insurance agent - who lived down the road from us - came over and the two of us stood up on the hill looking down into a gaping black hole which once was our home. I turned to him and said, "The Lord giveth and the Lord taketh away. Blessed be the name of the Lord.

Another vision God gave me was one in which I found myself standing in a large cave. Within the cave were many rooms with doors. Some doors were open and some were closed. I realized I was standing next to Jesus and we soon began to walk through this cave. Occasionally the Lord would stop and look into one of the many rooms

Eventually, we approached a large door which was secured with thick chains. The Lord looked at me and asked me what was kept behind that particular door. I knew the answer to His question, but I only replied that He didn't need to be concerned because I could take care of whatever it was.

Jesus left me at this point. I approached that chained door and decided to take a little peek inside. I possessed the keys to the door, but I only wanted to see inside a tiny bit, maybe just crack the door a little. As I cracked the door, there was a loud blast as the door blew open and out burst the ugliest demon anyone could ever imagine.

I had kept him in this secret place, trying to control him, but he was very powerful as he knocked me to the floor.

As I struggled to break free from that monster who was clawing at my insides, I cried out, "Jesus, save me from this evil spirit." Soon an angel of the Lord appeared next to me and that demon fled in terror. Jesus came to set the captives free and I was free indeed!

God declares in *Romans 8:38-39, "For I am convinced that neither death nor life, neither angels nor demons, neither the present nor the future, nor any powers, neither height nor depth, nor anything else in all creation, will be able to separate us from the love of God that is in Christ Jesus our Lord."*

I need to share one last story with you about my mother and the supernatural. For many years my mother and I had few communications. On one rare trip home, I encountered a supernatural visitation.

I was sitting next to her while she was laying on her bed. I heard these words come out of her mouth, "Do not Cast Me Out! Do no Cast Me Out! I do not want to throw up!"

May times while delivering people from demons they will throw up some phlegm.

Eventually, my parents retired to Florida. My father died and my mother became ill with dementia. As things progressed, we were called to her home to deal with her failing health. It was determined, for safety reasons, that she could not remain in her home alone.

We made the decision to moved her to our home in Missouri. Shortly after that, realizing we could not properly care for her we moved her to Senior facility that would give her the care she needed.

It was during this time that I had the privilege of leading my Mom to the Lord. Upon accepting Christ her whole character changed. She became more loving and cordial.

Christians are waging a tremendous battle against the forces of evil and we must be ever aware and vigilant.

John 8:32 states, *"Then you will know the truth, and the truth will set you free."*

CHAPTER EIGHTEEN
CAMPING

On a lighter note, I have been reflecting on some of our past camping experiences. My wife loved to go camping. Our budget was so tight in the early years of our marriage that we couldn't afford a tent so we would take the back seat out of our little Volkswagen Bug to sleep on. Our favorite camping spot was Lake Beardsley in Wisconsin. It was a beautiful, woodsy campground with a nicely stocked fishing lake.

After arriving there, my wife was expected to set up camp and watch the kids while I went fishing. She would always select what she thought was a great site, usually on the side of the hill, assuring us that any rainwater which poured down would wash right past us.

One time while on our way to Lake Beardsley, we stopped at a small gas station. As I was pumping gas, I noticed a large and looming thundercloud coming our way. The wind began to pick up and I figured a storm was imminent. After paying the gas station attendant, I jumped into our car and headed on down the road.

After a refreshing camping vacation, we decided to stop and gas up at the same filling station on our way back home. When I pulled up only one pump remained standing and the service building and all the house trailers in the trailer park situated next door were gone. The attendant came out of a small portable building that had been set up temporarily. The man remembered our family from when we had previously visited and bought gas and snacks. He said about two minutes after we left, the entire area was hit by a terrible tornado. In addition to destroying the station and all the homes in the trailer park, some people had been killed. I could not imagine what might have happened to us if we had tarried just a little longer. God has so graciously watched over and protected our family.

One of our camping adventures was a trip to Yellowstone National Park. We were pulling a pop-up camper which we borrowed from my mom and dad. Our vehicle at that time was a blue Chevy Nova which we purchased when we attended college in Michigan. After arriving at majestic Yellowstone Park, we found a nice site and set up camp. We were in awe of the great geyser, Old Faithful.

We were also happy to frequent the camp store where we purchased a canvas backpack and an ample supply of rich and gooey snacks. Because we didn't properly store our food, which was the rule, we were visited by a park bear and saw his tracks the next day.

It made us a little edgy and we concluded that although we were enjoying our getaway, we would head for home. We broke down our camp and packed up our camper.

Before we could snap down the last latch, we were hit by a torrent of rain. We were soaking wet from head to toe as we jumped into our vehicle.

In just a short time, we were driving on a narrow, curvy, mountainous road. From out of nowhere, a big, brown bear emerged. He came running straight toward us, acting like he wanted to infiltrate our car. Next, he began to run parallel to us, just like a dog chasing a car. It was like we were in a neck-to-neck race. Then just as suddenly as he had appeared, he turned and ran off. I guess he realized he could not outrun our hot, little Chevy.

Soon after we had another harrowing experience. Ruth and the kids had just gotten over our bear encounter and we were all a bit edgy. It was still very early in the morning when we went around a sharp curve. I saw a pile of rocks that had tumbled down the side of the mountain blocking our passage. The road was unduly slippery from all the rain. I was unable to stop so my only option was to head for the smallest boulders and hope I would not do too much damage to the undercarriage of our auto. On impact, we ground to a halt. We were surprised that the camper we were towing was still intact.

There had not been any traffic on this road for a long time and we were stranded and alone out in the middle of nowhere on high bear alert! It seemed like an eternity went by but in about thirty minutes, a pickup truck came up the road towards us. The driver was an accommodating young man who was on his way to work in the next town which was about seventy-five miles down the road.

We knew that we needed a tow truck because of the damage to our transmission.

Our new friend promised to send someone out to help us when he arrived in town. We settled in to wait. About three-hours later, we saw the most beautiful sight. Rumbling up the mountain was a large tow truck coming to our aid. Backing up to our car, he lifted the front to access the damaged transmission. One of the arms had been bent backward and he needed to disconnect the drive-shaft. My family piled into the car because his truck only could seat two.

When we finally arrived in town, we were taken to the Chevy garage and left there for repairs. I was so grateful to the tow truck operator and expressed my gratitude as I prepared to pay him for his services. I wondered how much a trek involving one hundred and fifty-miles round trip plus all the work involved in preparing our car to be towed would cost. I hoped I could pay him and still have enough money left for my car repairs. To my astonishment, he only charged us seventy-five dollars.

Another blessing came when the car mechanic said he would be able to bend the arm back so I could once again shift gears. In just a short time, we were back in our car and heading home where we arrived safely with no more incidents. Every time something adverse happened, God has always come through for us; even in the smallest things. It may not seem like a big deal but to us, it was.

One time we had a flat tire and were in a vicarious spot off the road and on a slope with a tire jack that was too short to lift our car.

I needed a miracle and right along the road and next to our vehicle were two lengths of 2x4 lumber. By putting them under our car jack, I was able to lift our car just enough to get the flat off and put on the spare.

This isn't the first time this has happened to me. One afternoon, we were driving to a neighboring town called Lebanon to eat at Captain D's. I decided to take a shortcut to the restaurant by going through a large parking lot. I heard God's Holy Spirit say that if I went that way, I would get a flat tire. I didn't take the spirit's warning and drove through anyway because I was in a hurry to get to the restaurant.

After arriving at our destination, I walked behind the car and noticed that one of my back tires was going flat. We quickly got into our car and drove to the nearest station. We were able to put some air in the tire, but it was not going to last long. On this vehicle, a Rav4, the spare tire was bolted to the back door.

I had open-heart surgery that summer and was not permitted to lift much weight. It was impossible to change the tire by myself. It was a Sunday afternoon so no place was open where we could get help. I noticed that behind the gas station was a small building. Above the door was a sign reading, "TOWING". Another sign located on the door read, "CLOSED SUNDAYS". God knew exactly what I needed and as we sat there, he sent a driver in a tow truck who pulled right up next to us.

I told him our predicament and he agreed to help us even though it was his day off. I had placed the jack under the wrong area of our car.

In a short time, he corrected my mistake and mounted our spare. I paid him the service charge which was only twenty-five dollars and thanked him for his help. These things don't happen by accident.

As I think about the many events which have happened in my life, I am overcome with emotion by the goodness of God as he has walked with me in my daily life. We face so many seasons in a lifetime and we experience so many changes as we walk along but he is always there to guide us.

CHAPTER NINETEEN
GRANNY AND EARL

I had a spectacular vision involving the salvation of an elderly gentleman I had the privilege to meet and lead to the Lord. It happened like this: One day, my wife was at the laundromat where she struck up a conversation with a young lady who was also doing her laundry. She told my wife, Ruth, her husband's grandmother lived nearby. She was a Christian but had little fellowship. Ruth said she would be happy to visit with that little old lady sometime.

After they finished their laundry, they headed down the street to meet Sally Weisman, the little old lady who preferred people just call her Granny. Ruth and Granny straight off became friends. Earl, Granny's husband, was there and was thrilled to share in the visit. Earl had an old fishing boat. He told Ruth he wanted to get rid of it and if I was interested, I should come to look at it. When Ruth told me this, we decided we would return to visit them together. Earl was a big man.

He was soft-spoken and cordial enough, but he did not appreciate Christianity. He could not understand it and did not want to hear about it. Granny told everyone not to mention Jesus around him and certainly not to say, "Praise the Lord" around him, because he considered himself to be atheist.

I am outspoken and did mention Jesus and say Praise the Lord in Earl's presence but I was also respectful of him. Over time we developed a great friendship and love for each other. One day, we received a call from Granny saying she was very sick. She wanted us to come by and pray for her, but she didn't want Earl to know because he wouldn't like it.

When we arrived at Granny's house, I told her Earl was the head of the home and that we needed to tell him why I was there. She reluctantly agreed. I entered the living room where Earl was sitting in his big, overstuffed chair, reading the paper. I told him because Granny was very sick, I would like his permission to pray for her. He looked up at me and said, "Why yes, of course."

Granny was sitting on a large couch next to the fireplace. I don't usually kneel to pray, but this time, I knelt next to the couch and invited Ruth and Granny to kneel with me. As I was praying, I suddenly felt a hand on my shoulder. I opened my eyes and looked up. Standing over me was Earl. His eyes were full of tears and he was weeping. I was so amazed and honored when he said, "John, would you mind if I knelt and prayed with you? I've never prayed for my wife." I said, "Absolutely". After we prayed, Earl got up and sat back in his chair.

I then went over to Earl and asked him if I could pray for him and he nodded his head yes.

I placed my hand on his bald head and began to pray silently. I suddenly felt a spirit of unbelief and commanded it to leave Earl. Then I prayed for God to save him.

Leaving for home, Ruth and I jumped into our Volkswagen Beetle and headed down the road. We didn't get too far before the strangest thing began to happen. The top of our car seemed to disappear. I looked straight up into heaven. I asked the Lord just what I was looking at. He said I was entering into the heavenly Jerusalem - the city of the living God where thousands upon thousands of angels were in joyful assembly. I saw the Lord. He was lifted up and all the angels were in joyful praise around His throne. The next words I heard were, "When one sinner repents, all God's angels rejoice.

I asked, "Did Earl just get saved?" The answer came back, "No, I am showing you a future event." About six months later, I was privileged to lead that dear, old man to the Lord and baptize him.

CHAPTER TWENTY
MY HEART CONDITION

I have had three heart surgeries in my lifetime and God has shown me His love and power through all of them. My first surgery was a four-way bypass.

After a week in the hospital, I was sent home to recover. On my second day at home, I went into the bathroom and became light headed, fainted and fell to the floor. Lying there, I found myself in heaven in the presence of God. I looked back and realized that the door I had just entered through was closing. I asked God what I was experiencing. He told me he wanted to show me what happens when one of His saints dies and enters heaven.

He showed me that He will erase our memories of a loved one who does not make it into the heavenly eternity. We will never need to grieve for them.

Later, I found and read *Isaiah 65:17 which says, "See, I will create new heavens and a new earth. The former things will not be remembered, nor will they come to mind."*

Ruth realized I had fallen and called an ambulance to take me to the hospital. It was determined my heart was in A-fib.

I was given medicine for the arterial fibrillation, but it proved ineffective. I was told if it didn't correct itself, I would get electrical cardioversion, which absorbs the heart and restores a normal heart rate.

On Sunday morning, God touched me. I was hooked up to a large monitor screen showing my erratic heartbeat. I had just finished sharing with one of the nurses some of the many miracles God had done in my life. She said she had never experienced a miracle. After she left the room around 10 am, while lying in my bed, I sensed a supernatural occurrence. I saw something swoop down from the corner of the room. I felt it pass over me like a gentle wind. I sprung up and sat on the edge of the bed.

Just then, the nurse entered my room. "Oh my God, oh my God", she was yelling as she pointed to the monitor. "Look, look, the monitor is showing your heart is back to normal." She was so excited she almost tripped over the little table at the end of my bed. I was excited too. I looked at her and said, "You have just witnessed your first miracle". I have never experienced A-fib again.

I am reminded of Psalm 23:4 - *"Even though I walk through the darkest valley, I will fear no evil, for you are with me; your rod and your staff, they comfort me."*

My second heart surgery came five-years later. I needed an aortic valve replacement and was told the procedure should be done soon.

Of course, I prayed for God to heal me. Many of my Christian brothers and sisters prayed for me. I went forward at church and had the leadership pray for my healing. God had a different plan. It was to use a surgeon at Mercy Hospital in Springfield, Missouri.

My surgery was complicated and difficult. My family was unsure whether I would survive. On the second day after the surgery, I regained consciousness. When I opened my eyes, I could see a shadowy figure standing beside my bed. He was a tall, skinny man dressed in a shiny black polyester suit.

I instantaneously recognized him and knew it was Satan himself. He sneered at me and in a mocking tone, he hissed, "Well John, what do you think of the situation you find yourself in now?" I smugly replied, "Devil, it all comes with the territory." After that, he vanished and never returned.

Although the days following the second surgery were rough, I never questioned God or asked Him why he allowed me to endure this ordeal. God always has a perfect plan for those who love Him. He never left me in the dark when facing any situation. One morning while I was resting in my bed, I heard the Holy Spirit speaking to me. Often when God's spirit is speaking to me, He calls me by my name.

On that morning, He said, "John, do you remember the story when I called the Israelites out of Babylon and returned them to Israel?" " One of the things they did was to rebuild the walls", he explained. "A man named Nehemiah was commissioned by Me to repair the breaches in the walls. I could have called angels to rebuild the breaches in those walls, but instead, I chose a man. You had a breach in your wall and I chose a man to repair it." God has always wonderfully supplied all my needs. His goodness and mercy have surely followed me all the days of my life. I can't help but weep as I pen these words.

As I share my story, I am awestruck by the amazing God we

serve. He has wonderfully intervened in my life so many times. God never wastes our experiences with Him but uses them for our good.

One More Miracle occurred on Friday, March 12, 2021. Our son, Eric, had just been released from the hospital. He had become so weak he could barely walk. We all thought he caught the Covid-19 virus.

Eric's wife, Lisa, made him an appointment to be tested. By the time he was going he could barely get into the car. Unbeknownst to him he was standing at death's door.

He did not have the virus, but severe blood loss. Fortunately, the nurse in attendance recognized the symptoms. He had fatigue, weakness, pale skin and dizziness. Someone can go into shock hemorrhaging when they have lost 20 percent or more of their total blood volume. Once you have lost 50 percent of your total volume, your heart will stop pumping. He was so fatigued, he was moments away from entering into a coma.

The nurse was unhesitant in calling the paramedics who transported him to our local hospital. An adult male has about twelve pints of blood, Eric only had four pints.
At the hospital he was given three blood transfusions. This saved his life. Praise be to the Lord! Eric has recovered and is now safely home. God has always gloriously cared for our family.

CHAPTER TWENTY-ONE
MY FAMILY

After our house burnt to the ground we relocated to Osage Beach. One day, the Lord spoke to me, saying, "I want you to leave the strip and relocate your business to your home."

I talked to my dear wife about this and she agreed, asking where I wanted to set it up. "How about in the living room?", I replied, and so it was. Our grassy front yard became a gravel parking lot. All the furniture came out of the living room and was replaced with showcases and displays. Our two-car garage became part of our business as well as a room we build to house fine jewelry and jewelry repair.

At this writing, that location know as KK Jewelers still exists. We are located on Hwy KK in Osage Beach, Missouri.
I know I have been blessed with a full life, filled with awesome experiences and some amazing people.

Most importantly, God has blessed me with a very special family. I give much credit to my wife, Ruth. She has always been the heart of our home.

My two children, Carla and Eric are adults now. My daughter, Carla, has become a cracker jack real estate agent. My son, Eric, is the jeweler at our store. He is very talented and successful in his industry. I am extremely proud of their accomplishments and so pleased with the kind and caring individuals they have become.

I have six grandchildren and two great-grandchildren. My daughter, Carla, raised two fine, young men, Chase and Creed. My son, Eric, did a great job with his four children, Kyle, Lindsey, Christopher and Tyler. All my grandchildren are amazing, young adults. A tremendous amount of love exists between all of us.

I am blessed with two of the cutest, most lively great-grandchildren anyone could hope for. They are Luna and Jude. They are the children of my granddaughter, Lindsey. They add so much to our family whenever they visit.

EPILOGUE
A GREAT HOPE

Psalms 32:7 -- " *You are my hiding place; you will protect me from trouble and surround me with sons of deliverance.*"

Revelations 22:20 - "*He who testifies to these things says, "Yes, I am coming soon.*" Amen. Come, Lord Jesus!

I now find myself in the latter years of my life. Some day we're all going to die but I am looking forward to participating in this great event. God has brought me and my family this far. The Bible tells us that every good thing in our life is a gift from God. Nothing that I have accomplished have I done on my own. Everything I hoped to achieve, God achieved for me and my family.

I can without hesitation, call them miracles from God's own hand. His grace is displayed in my life every day. If only I could return this great love, he has shown for us. It seems like yesterday I opened my eyes to this old world. Eighty-one years seems like only a small grain of sand on all the beaches around the world.

I sometimes wonder what eternity will be like. I know I have already started my walk-through eternity and believe that it started when God created me in my mother's womb. He then called me into His kingdom through His Son, Jesus Christ.

He put His Spirit in me and changed my life forever. Many who know me can testify to this miracle.

John: 4:13 - "*And if I go and prepare a place for you, I will come back and take you to be with me that you also may be where I am."*

My life has been a wonderful journey. I will never regret my choice to follow Christ.

Hebrews: 11:8 - *"By faith Abraham, when called to go to a place he would later receive as his inheritance, obeyed and went, even though he did not know where he was going."*

Living by Faith My Last Thoughts

Hebrews 11:6 - *"And without faith it is impossible to please God, because anyone who comes to him must believe that he exists and that he rewards those who earnestly seek him."*

When I heard God's voice say, John receive my son, Jesus, " I immediately responded, "Yes, Lord." That was the greatest supernatural experience that I have ever encountered. At that moment my whole life changed. Just as God revealed Himself to Abraham and made a covenant with him, God made a covenant with me and my family. It has become a covenant of blessings. He led our family to the promise land.

Matthew 6:33 - *"But seek first his kingdom and his righteousness, and all these things will be given to you as well."*

As I was writing my story, I was looking out at the beautiful Lake of the Ozarks. A place God gave to us. One of my life's desires was to live on a lake. The business God told me to start has become a fantastic financial blessing. Through it we have been able to bless others.

2 Corinthians 9:8-9 - *"And God is able to bless you abundantly, so that in all things at all times, having all that you need, you will abound in every good work. As it is written: "They have freely scattered their gifts to the poor; their righteousness endures forever."*

Because of Him we have been debt free for years. This is not about me, it is about God's grace in our life. It is a divine influence which operates in all who call upon the Lord.

My life's story is almost over. It has been a glorious trip looking back at my life. I'm excitingly looking forward to meeting the King of Glory, whether here or in Heaven. In any case, it will be a glorious time. I hope to see you there.

God bless you all. I pray the story of my life may touch someone's heart and you may come to know my Lord and Savior if you don't already know Him.

Life is Too Short

by John Kenyon

Life is too short to miss heaven.
This life will soon pass away.
Our Lord will be coming back,
His glory to display.
Life is too short to miss heaven.
Let us all kneel down and pray.
Life is too short to miss heaven.
He is coming back someday.

BIBLIOGRAPHY

These are the bible verses that are quoted throughout the book. Quotes are from the NIV Bible translation.

"We know that we are children of God and that the whole world is under the control of the evil one" – 1 John 5:19

"For what shall it profit a man if he gains the whole world, and loses his own soul?" – Mark 8:36

The Lord is my shepherd, I lack nothing. He makes me lie down in green pastures, he leads me beside quiet waters, he refreshes my soul. He guides me along the right paths for his name's sake. Even though I walk through the darkest valley,

I will fear no evil, for you are with me; your rod and your staff, they comfort me.

You prepare a table before me in the presence of my enemies. You anoint my head with oil; my cup overflows. Surely your goodness and love will follow me all the days of my life, and I will dwell in the house of the Lord forever. -- Psalm 23

"Many, O Lord my God, are the wonders you have done. The things you planned for us no one can recount to you; were I to speak and tell of your deeds, they would be too many to declare." -- Psalms 40:5

_____

"We will not hide from their children, but tell to the coming generations the glorious deeds of the Lord, and His might and wonders that he has done." -- Psalms 78:4

_____

"But you will receive power when the Holy Spirit comes upon you." -- Acts 1:8

_____

"The steps of a good man are ordered by the Lord and He delights in his ways." – Psalm 37:23

_____

"But God hath revealed them unto us by His Spirit for the Spirit searches all things, yea, the deep things of God." – 1 Corinthians 2:10

_____

"Trust in the Lord with all your heart and lean not on your understanding; in all ways acknowledge him, and he shall direct your paths." -- Proverbs 3:5-6

_____

"Ask and it will be given to you; seek and you will find; knock and the door will be opened to you." -- Matthew 7:7

_____

"A man's heart plans his way, but the Lord directs his steps." – Proverbs 16:9

_____

"If you forgive anyone's sins, their sins are forgiven; if you don't forgive them, they are not forgiven. Therefore, we are ambassadors for Christ, as though God were making his appeal through us." -- 2 Corinthians 5:20

_____

"who knows if the spirit of a man rises upward and if the spirit of the animal goes down into the earth." -- Ecclesiastes 3:21

_____

"There was a rich man who was dressed in purple and fine linen and lived in luxury every day. At his gate was laid a beggar named Lazarus, covered with sores and longing to eat what fell from the rich man's table. Even the dogs came and licked his sores.

"The time came when the beggar died and the angels carried him to Abraham's side. The rich man also died and was buried. In Hades, where he was in torment, he looked up and saw Abraham far away, with Lazarus by his side. So he called to him, 'Father Abraham, have pity on me and send Lazarus to dip the tip of his finger in water and cool my tongue, because I am in agony in this fire.'

"But Abraham replied, 'Son, remember that in your lifetime you received your good things, while Lazarus received bad things, but now he is comforted here and you are in agony. And besides all this, between us and you a great chasm has been set in place, so that those who want to go from here to you cannot, nor can anyone cross over from there to us.'

"He answered, 'Then I beg you, father, send Lazarus to my family, for I have five brothers. Let him warn them, so that they will not also come to this place of torment.'

"Abraham replied, 'They have Moses and the Prophets; let them listen to them.'

"'No, father Abraham,' he said, 'but if someone from the dead goes to them, they will repent.'

"He said to him, 'If they do not listen to Moses and the Prophets, they will not be convinced even if someone rises from the dead.'" -- Luke 16:19-31

"You shall know them by their fruits. Do men gather grapes from thorn bushes or figs from thistles? Even so, every good tree bears good fruit, but a bad tree bears bad fruit. A good tree cannot bear bad fruit, nor can a bad tree bear good fruit. Every tree that does not bear fruit is cut down and thrown into the fire. Therefore, by their fruits, you will know them." -- --Matthew 7:16-20

"They triumphed over him by the blood of the Lamb and by the word of their testimony; they did not love their lives so much as to shrink from death." -- Revelation 12:1

"My prayer is not that you take them out of the world but that you protect them from the evil one." -- John 17:15

Then Jesus asked him, "What is your name?" "My name is Legion, for we are many." – Mark 5:9

"And these signs shall follow them that believe; In my name shall they cast out demons..." – Mark 16:17

"Do you know that you yourselves are God's temple, and now the Spirit of God dwells in your?" -- 1 Corinthians 3:16

"My temple will be called a house of prayer, but you have turned it into a den of thieves." -- Matthew 21:13

"For he will command his angels concerning you to guard you in all your ways." -- Psalm 91:11

"I trust in you; do not let me be put to shame, nor let my enemies triumph over me." -- Psalm 25:2

"See, I will create new heavens and a new earth. The former things will not be remembered, nor will they come to mind." -- Isaiah 65:17

"For I am convinced that neither death nor life, neither angels nor demons, neither the present nor the future, nor any powers, neither height nor depth, nor anything else in all creation, will be able to separate us from the love of God that is in Christ Jesus our Lord." -- Romans 8:38-39

"Then you will know the truth, and the truth will set you free." -- John 8:32

"He will also keep you firm to the end, so that you will be blameless on the day of our Lord Jesus Christ." -- 1 Corinthians 1:8

"In their hearts humans play their course, but the Lord establishes their steps." -- Proverbs 16:9

"And if I go and prepare a place for you, I will come back and take you to be with me that you also may be where I am." --John 4:13

"By faith Abraham, when called to go to a place he would later receive as his inheritance, obeyed and went, even though he did not know where he was going." -- Hebrews 11:8

"And without faith it is impossible to please God, because anyone who comes to him must believe that he exists and that he rewards those who earnestly seek him." -- Hebrew 11:6

"But seek first his kingdom and his righteousness, and all these things will be given to you as well." -- Matthew 6:33

"And God is able to bless you abundantly, so that in all things at all times, having all that you need, you will abound in every good work. As it is written: "They have freely scattered their gifts to the poor; their righteousness endures forever." -- 2 Corinthians 9:8-9

" You are my hiding place; you will protect me from trouble and surround me with sons of deliverance. -- Psalm 32:7

"He who testifies to these things says, "Yes, I am coming soon." -- Revelations 22:20

Check out John's teachings at

DIRECTIVESFORDISCIPLES@LIVE

and Check out John's Facebook page also called

Directives for Disciples.